CONSEQUENC

IF THE WHALES CAN'T SURVIVE
NEITHER CAN WE

Sue Cross

***

***

1

ALSO BY SUE CROSS

On The Menu: Animal Welfare
An A to Z of How Farm Animals Live and Die
All Aboard The Laughter Bus

CONTENTS

"Water and air, the two essential fluids on which all life depends, have become global garbage cans."

Oceanographer Jacques-Yves Cousteau

1

The Cruel Plastic Sea

"Only we humans make waste that nature can't digest."
Charles Moore, Marine Researcher

Scarface is back from a dive that has lasted nearly an hour. Blowing through his S-shaped blowhole he is clearing out his lungs, getting rid of carbon dioxide and recharging his oxygen supply. Like all sperm whales he is a deep-sea diver of supreme proportions and consummate efficiency. And the largest toothed predator on Earth.

The way his body adapts to his dives is awe-inspiring. Pumping his flukes up and down in a steady rhythm, he glides ever deeper: three and a half miles an hour; five hundred and fifty feet a minute. As he goes down his lungs and ribcage deflate; other internal organs compress, and some close down. His spermcaceti organ - that spans the top of his head - begins to solidify to match the denseness of the water.

The only other mammal (and the only other vertebrate) that dives deeper than a sperm whale is the elusive Cuvier's beaked whale. No other mammals can withstand the pressure, a weight that every ten metres becomes one atmosphere heavier. At one thousand metres deep it's almost one hundred atmospheres - an unimaginable crushing force.

That was the depth of Scarface's dive and where he had found what he was looking for: a giant squid. Weighing four hundred and fifty pounds and forty foot in length - if you include the tentacles - it had made a good meal, and a formidable adversary. Although - as if these giants weren't challenge enough – the colossal squid, the super-sized version, is his preferred choice. About double the size of the giant squid the colossal squid's body measures forty feet. Its eight arms of different lengths, but three feet on average, and two, six foot long tentacles, adds to its length; and at about eleven hundred pounds, this monstrous squid is as heavy as an elephant seal. Scarface has to dive down six or seven thousand feet for one of those; well over a mile and a dive that lasts well over an hour. Down to where the temperature is a constant $4\,°C$, the darkness total, the water calm and the pressure about two hundred atmospheres.

It was this leviathan, the colossal squid, that had given Scarface his name. He already had the big sucker marks to prove his confrontation with the giant squid. The sharp discs on its suckers had dug in and gripped hard. But the colossal squid has weapons that are more gruesome still. It was Scarface's first encounter with one of these that has marked him most. Like hellacious weapons the squid's vicious suckers - sharp-hooked and some of those three-pointed - had bitten into him. They did damage enough. But worse still were some of the twenty-five rotating hooks at the end of each of the squid's two longer feeding tentacles. Like an abundance of hideous power drills the squid had ground into him.

But now he has perfected his hunting technique. The world's largest toothed predator against the world's largest invertebrate. Scarface, the size of a Boeing 737, against a quarry the weight of a hefty beef steer. A fight to the death, the death of the squid.

The battle won, Scarface opens his mouth wide, a mouth which, being completely under his head and relatively narrow, is quite unlike the jaw of any other whale (and seems as peculiar as a human having a mouth under the chin). The size of his mouth is also surprising. It seems a relatively insubstantial opening for a head of such vast capacity, a head that makes up one third of his body mass. Scarface opened his mouth wide and with a mighty gulp swallowed the vast animal in one piece, the whole ton of it. No need to chew - the first part of his four-chambered stomach would grind it up. It would have been no use bringing this meal up to the surface. As the water pressure eased, the gases in the squid's body would have begun to decompress and form bubbles before dissolving into a gloopy, unmanageable mess.

On average Scarface's dives last forty-minutes, though some last over an hour and a half with two hours being just about his limit. As he comes to the surface, his stomach full and his hunt over, his blood circulation warms his spermaceti and it begins to match the density of the surface water. Then, through his single blow hole that is near the front of his head and slightly to the left, he sends his blow fifteen feet up into the air at, if the weather is calm, an angle of forty-five degrees. And then, old, stale air and carbon dioxide expelled, he replenishes his lungs with a fresh supply of oxygen.

But Scarface's lungs are not his only oxygen repository. Like all great whales they take up just three percent of his abdominal cavity (humans' lungs take up seven per cent of theirs). His other important iron store is hemoglobin, the oxygen carrying cells that make blood red. In whales hemoglobin accounts for about sixty per cent of their blood content (in human blood it's thirty per cent) a refinement that keeps him supplied with oxygen during long dives.

For all the hazards the risks of diving deep for a colossal squid are well worth it. A super-size meal in one dive is a much better pay-off than many lesser dives and smaller prey. For Scarface, like all sperm whales, needs calories by the ton, one ton a day, three per cent of his body weight. But not all of the squid converts to calories. Squids' parrot-like beaks are made of one the hardest materials found in nature: chitin, exclusive to arthropods and the stuff that the exoskeletons of crustaceans and insects are made of. Not surprisingly they are indigestible and need to be got rid off. Sometimes vomiting does the trick. But very occasionally squid beaks work their way down to the lower part of sperm whales' three hundred metre intestines. Then ambergris, a thick, black, foul smelling liquid, forms. It eases the passage of the beaks either up and out, through the mouth. Or down, and out, through the anus.

Scarface knows that squid have a keen sense of smell (though he himself does not). He knows that its eyes - which are the largest in the world, and at least as large as a human head - are so efficient they have excellent vision even in the bioluminescence of the ocean depths where all sorts of organisms glow in the darkness, from bacteria and worms to fish. The fish include the one and a half foot cookie-cutter sharks whose glowing underbellies lure unsuspecting animals and give these weirdest of sharks a chance to gouge a bite of flesh.

Scarface also knows that, thanks to his biosonar, he can track squid as effectively as the squid tracks its own prey. His echo soundings are similar to phenomenally loud hammering, sort of super clicks, that he usually only makes when he is hunting (female sperm whales make similar hunting sounds but theirs are distinctive to their pod). At other times Scarface occasionally squeals and trumpets, but it is his hunting clicks, that last only a fraction of a second, that are the loudest – and the loudest animal sound on Earth. He knows he can outwit his target because what the squid can't do is sense Scarface's low frequency echolocating reports even though they reach two hundred and thirty decibels, a sound so powerful it would destroy human eardrums and shake a human to death.

It's easy to imagine that Scarface's hunting ground - a mile and a quarter below the surface where the abyssal zone begins - is pristine and untouched by human interference. But that would be wrong. Man-made garbage is not just in the ocean shallows and on continental shelves. It has also found its way into the oceans' deepest canyons, its darkest depths, where some animals, like the colossal squid, grow to immense proportions. Even in Earth's most remote places the muck and litter from human life is accumulating, driven by deep ocean currents that have funnelled it there.

Using the oceans as a rubbish tip is nothing new. The clinker from the days of steamships still lies deep down on ocean floors. This was, of course, tipped out with other waste. But that other waste, being organic, has long since decomposed. Today's debris and industrial waste is very different Most is inorganic, made from petroleum-based synthetic polymers, and known as plastic.

Plastic. The most abundant form of solid-waste pollution on earth. Invented in 1855 and first mass-produced in the1950s. It's lethal stuff. Chemically inert. Non-biodegradable. Unnatural. The only way it changes is in size - into ever smaller pieces until, eventually, those pieces become microscopic. And no less deadly.

It seems very little is plastic-free these days. And of all the plastic that has ever been made ten per cent is now in the oceans. Either put there on purpose. Or accidentally spilled. Or dumped illegally.

Most of this imperishable detritus, but by no means all, comes from the land, out of landfills, towns, cities and farmland, from where the rivers carry it to the seas. It's a vast, assortment: polythene from food, drink and toiletry packaging. Disposable cups made from Styrofoam. PVC plumbing pipes and shower curtains. Polyester clothing. Nylon binding straps. Petrol cans and oil drums. Silicone sealants, silicone insulation, silicone oils. Toys. Balloons. Balls. Cars. Furniture. Furnishings. Micro-pellets used in abrasive cleaners and as exfoliants in cosmetics. Industrial waste. Medical waste. Endless types of waste.

Of the other plastic that ends up on beaches and in the oceans four-fifths comes from the land and the rest from shipping: from cargo ships, fishing boats, pleasure boats; from offshore rigs and from containers lost at sea. Every year hundreds of containers fall off ships, but that number turns into thousands if the cargo that is lost when ships sink or go aground is included. All manner of twenty-first century objects lost: toys, motorbikes, computers, sports gear, clothing, carpets, kitchen ware, industrial machinery. The list is long.

In the oceans opportunist and indiscriminate feeders swallow whatever comes their way. Balls from roll-on deodorant bottles and ping-pong balls are mistaken for turtle eggs. Nurdles (tiny pre-production plastic pellets that are used in the manufacture of other plastics and transported all over the world) look like fish eggs and plankton.

In the centre of the North Pacific, Midway Atoll couldn't be further from man's plastic-dependent society. Yet nearly all of the one and a half million Laysan Albatross that live there have plastic in their digestive systems and one third of their chicks die. They have been found dead, stuffed with objects made from plastic including sweet wrappers, synthetic string and Styrofoam.

In the1960s it was calculated that five per cent of seabirds had some plastic in their stomachs. By 1980 that figure had risen to eighty per cent. Now it's ninety percent.

For those who feed randomly supermarket plastic bags are particularly lethal. Dolphins and sea turtles, and tuna, sharks and swordfish, are among those who mistake them for jellyfish. Just one bag can block breathing passages and digestive tracts. Filter feeders like the great baleen whales scoop them up. And suction feeders, like sperm and beaked whales, who suck up their prey in great gulps, are particularly vulnerable to large pieces of plastic debris. The proof of their demise is evident from autopsies on whales washed up all over the world.

On Spain's south coast a thirty-two foot sperm whale had been killed by an obstruction in its digestive system. The blockage had been caused by fifty-nine different plastic items; altogether they weighed thirty-seven pounds. Most of the plastic was transparent sheeting, probably from the so-called 'Costa del Polythene' (the small coastal plain of Campo de Dalias) in south eastern Spain which covers twenty-six thousand hectares and is the world's largest concentration of greenhouses. The whale's stomach contents included nine meters of rope, two lengths of hosepipe, two small flowerpots, a spray canister and, as nearly always, supermarket bags: the bags that harm sperm whales more than any other creature.

When two dead sperm whales were washed up on the Californian coast it was found that one had died from a burst stomach, ruptured by some of the four hundred and fifty pounds of synthetic litter, including fishing nets, in its guts. The digestive tract of its half-starved fellow had been blocked by a wad of plastic.

The plastic that filled the stomachs of seven sperm whales found dead on Italy's Adriatic coast included ropes and fishing lines with hooks attached.

Off France's Normandy coast a dead minke whale was found to have nearly a ton of plastic -at least one tenth of own her weight – in her stomach, including the oceans' ubiquitous plastic bags.

The intestines' of a Brydes's whale washed up near Cairns in Australia had been clogged with towels, surgical gloves, plastic pieces, duct tape, sweat pants and a golf ball.

One thousand pieces of plastic - including one hundred and fifteen cups, four bottles, twenty five plastic bags, two flipflops and one nylon sack – was the tally of the stomach contents of a 31ft sperm whale washed up on Indonesia's east coast.

But most dead whales - and most dead marine animals - don't wash up on shores. Their death toll can only be imagined for where prey is plentiful and animals feed, plastic junk is often plentiful too.

Anything that floats – like pieces of plastic, marine animals and vegetation - can be driven by rotating winds and currents into convergence zones, or gyres. Since the centre of a gyre tends to remain calm anything that has been carried there – particularly if it is inanimate - becomes trapped by the gyres' circulating currents.

Every ocean has one. There are gyres in the Indian Ocean; in the North and the South Atlantic Oceans; and in the South Pacific Ocean. But the best known is in the centre of the North Pacific, between California and Hawaii. This is the Pacific Trash Vortex that is also known as the Great Pacific Garbage Patch, the one that the media so often become enthused about. Driven by winds and tides it takes six years for the junk from North America's west coast - the plastics, the chemical sludge and all the other jettisoned man-made debris - to reach it. But the rubbish from the east coast of Asia can get there in less than a year.

For over three years the Ocean Cleanup Foundation and six universities carried out a survey of the Pacific Vortex using two aircraft and thirty vessels. Their findings, published in 2018, showed that the area of the trash gyre was sixteen times greater than their previous estimate; that it's range was over seven hundred and twenty thousand square miles (three times the area of France); and contained seventy-nine thousand tonnes of debris. Twenty per cent of that refuse was from the 2011 Japanese tsunami; and almost almost half was discarded fishing nets. The authors of the study described the growth of all this detritus as exponential. In other words this is rubbish that will keep mounting up, and at an ever increasing rate.

As plastic debris floats on the surface it begins to take on a sulphurous fishy stench. For some seabirds this rotten-egg smell is a signal that food is available. Those who show a particular interest are petrels and albatrosses who only come to land to rear their young (and it's thought, though it hasn't been been proved, that they also sleep, as well as eat, on the wing). And so, rather than their natural diet of fish, molluscs and cephalopods – like squid and octopus - they fill their stomachs with bottle caps, cigarette lighters, toothbrushes, buttons, small balls and toys, and a mass of other small plastic pieces. With no space left for proper food, they starve to death.

But most plastic that arrives in the oceans is not as visible as we might imagine. It does not show up on satellite imagery. Most is not even visible to the naked eye - for the ocean's surface is not the final resting place for mankind's discarded synthetic materials. Only ten percent, the most recently arrived objects, float on the surface: the debris that is in the first stage of breaking into smaller parts. By some calculations the oceans' surface plastic is equivalent to the weight of fifteen hundred blue whales (three hundred thousand tons) .

Its reduction into insidious particles is relentless. Once in the oceans it enters an unstoppable phase as plastic fragments render into ever smaller pieces. Never will they decompose as organic materials decompose. No microorganisms will transform them into anything beneficial the way bacteria - the oceans' main decomposers - break down organic waste into nutrients that nourish marine life. Instead, all this synthetic material will become smaller and smaller until, eventually, it is reduced to tiny particles, a kind of inanimate plankton: 'microplastics' (a term coined in 2014 by marine biologist Professor Richard Thompson of the UK's Plymouth University).

About ninety percent of all the oceans' plastic is in microplastic form. Invisible to the naked eye and impossible to remove, suspended beneath the surface these specks of plastic fill water columns down to the sea bed, down to the deep sea sediments. And so the sand and mud on the ocean floor has become a sink for plastics of microscopic proportions. Smaller than five millimetres (one grain of sand measures between 0.06mm and 2mm) these microscopic plastic particles will not decay in any meaningful time-scale.

Decomposition of these unnatural materials is a process so slow that it spans hundreds of years. In landfills plastic bottles will take over four hundred years to rot away, and plastic bags about one thousand. But in water it's different. Even degradable materials break down more slowly in water than on land and the colder and deeper the water the longer decomposition takes. That helps explain why, for instance, in the Mid-Atlantic Ridge – one thousand, two hundred and fifty miles from land and nearly three miles deep - the bottles, plastic bags and fishing gear that have been discovered there will take an inordinately long time before they fracture into smaller pieces.

Even on the surface it takes time for plastics to weather and break up - enough time for alien species to hitch a ride across the oceans. Two years after the 2011 tsunami hit eastern Japan - when millions of objects, including entire fishing boats and buildings were jettisoned into the north Pacific Ocean - Hawaiian scientists found some of the wreckage on their beaches. And on that wreckage they discovered - still alive - two hundred and eighty-nine species. Most were invertebrates and most of those were molluscs; others included worms and crustaceans. Travelling at one or two knots across the Pacific they had taken two years to get there. During that long, slow journey some had even reproduced – which shows how some species are able to adapt to change.

Some plastics arrive in the oceans already in microplastic form, such as flecks of synthetic fabrics that have rubbed off during laundering; or fragments of pile hoovered from carpets; or pieces abraded from car tyres; or flakes of paint from road markings; or fragments mixed in the sludge that drains out of rubbish dumps. They are all part of the myriad of plastic particles that are carried to the seas by runoff. And some are already in the oceans - like flecks of marine paints, fragments from fishing nets and chips off surfboards. Endless types of tiny particles of synthetic waste, including nurdles.

Nurdles, the raw material of the manufacturing industries, are tiny pellets one to five millimetres in diameter that are transported all over the world. They leak from delivery trucks into streets, and from there into storm drains that take them down to the oceans. It has been estimated that ten per cent of the plastic litter on the world's beaches could be made up of these tiny nurdles, each the size of a lentil. And it's possible that seventy-three per cent of the sand on UK's beaches contains some too.

As plastic pieces break up into ever smaller fragments the more their surface area increases and the more hazardous they become. Not only do they emit the toxic chemicals that were used in their manufacture, but they absorb other pollutants, and the most commonly used plastics absorb the most.

The spread of poisonous chemicals is relentless and far reaching. The smaller the particles become the smaller the animals that ingest them, from tiny crustaceans to marine worms; and filter feeders from sponges to the great baleen whales. In this way their range becomes wider and their environmental impact greater. They have even reached the most remote parts of Earth.

Chemical compounds, like PCBs, can disrupt hormones. Synthesised insecticides (like DDT, the world's most powerful pesticide) have killed all manner of animals as they worked their way up the food chain. Although both of these chemical compounds were banned by most countries in the1970s DDT is so persistent that it's said there is not a single organism in the world that does not contain at least a trace. But for BPA. a main component of everyday hard wearing plastic - like sports bottles, baby bottles, food storage containers and the lining of food tins - there is no similar prohibition even though exposure to low doses has been linked to cardiovascular problems in humans.

In 2017 researchers used a robotic submarine to capture tiny scavenging crustaceans almost seven miles deep in the Mariana Trench, east of the Philippines. They found these tiny creatures were contaminated with fifty times more toxic chemicals than crabs in China's heavily polluted rivers. The pollutants included PCBs, once widely used as coolants in fridges, and PBDEs, once universal flame retardants, and both banned in the 1970s. The only way these toxic chemicals could have been absorbed by the scavenging crustaceans was through microplastics. The story is the same four thousand three hundred miles away north of New Zealand in the KermadecTrench.

It's said that one quarter of all fish now contain some plastic which means the potentially lethal chemicals are on their way up the food chain, up to the top, to whales and humans – and Puget Sound's orcas.

The killer whales that live along the north western coast of the US's Washington State are among the most contaminated marine mammals in the world. They feed mainly on Chinook salmon, about five hundred pounds a day. But these fish are contaminated by the outflows of toxins from the US's west coast industries. High levels of industrial-strength fire-retardent chemicals have weakened the orcas' immune systems; several of the man-made chemicals are carcinogenic; and toxins from heavy metals, such as lead, mercury, arsenic and cadmium, have the potential to damage nervous systems. As heavy metals can be excreted only very slowly they tend to build up over time. Known as bioaccumulation, or biomagnification - when toxic substances accumulate at a greater rate than they are lost – means the longer an animal lives the more poisoned they become.

The orcas' numbers have become so low that their status is now 'endangered' - and no-one seems optimistic about their future. It's looking as if in one hundred years the killer whales of Puget Sound will be no more.

Another great hazard for the residents of the marine world is fishing gear. It's said that twenty per cent of all the oceans' synthetic debris comes from the fishing industry, though, given the immense extent of the ocean environment it's impossible to be sure. It could be much more.

Once fishing nets were made from organic, biodegradable hemp. But since the 1950s this natural material has been replaced by artificial polyamides, better known as nylon. As a result all kinds of fishing gear – from nets to buoys to ropes – that are lost at sea might remain in their original condition for centuries.

Drift nets can be especially lethal. With floats at the top and weights at the bottom they hang like vast curtains in the high seas; the longest stretch for over fifty miles. Although they are intended to catch commercial fish like herring, tuna, squid and salmon they inevitably kill more than their intended targets. Invariably air-breathing sea mammals and birds get caught in them too – and their broken jaws and beaks are evidence of their struggle to escape. It 's estimated that in the Pacific Ocean alone about twenty thousand miles of drift nets are set out at any one time - some legally, others not.

Invariably some nets get lost; but still they continue to fish. Eventually the weight of whatever has been caught forces them to sink to the ocean floor. On the seabed scavengers gorge on the carcasses until the net, lightened of its load, rises again to resume its grisly mission. Not for nothing is this ghoulish quest called ghost fishing.

'Longlines' have hundreds – or even thousands - of short lines with baited hooks attached. They are set to catch tuna, shark, halibut and swordfish. The longest stretch for seventy miles. And, like fishing nets, they too trap seabirds and sea mammals who, having swallowed the hook, become trapped under water, and drown.

But all nets - trawl nets, bag-shaped nets, tangle nets, gill nets, that trap fish by their gills - all take their toll. It's estimated that every year fishing gear kills at least three hundred thousand cetaceans; hundreds of thousands of sea birds; a quarter of a million sea turtles and doubtless – though it's impossible to even estimate - a huge number of other marine animals, including seals, sea lions and penguins .

Over the last ten years more plastic has been produced than during the whole of last century, a rate of production that is predicted to double over the next fifteen years. Ellen MacArthurs Foundation warns that, if we continue producing plastic at the present rate, by 2050 the plastic content of the ocean will outweigh fish. Plastic everywhere. Including the digestive systems of marine animals.

Now that Scarface is in his twenties he travels the oceans alone, for strong bonds are not his forte. In his younger days, when he was ten years old and had just left the pod, he teamed up with Chrome and Echo. But the older the three whales grew the more solitary they preferred to be. Now the closest they get to others is when they join up with female pods to mate. By now Scarface has fathered several calves, a fact that interests him not at all. His most pressing concerns are migrating to the Arctic to hunt and feed in summer, and his return journey to warmer seas to mate in winter. A mating season and a feeding season and no-one but himself to be concerned about. The distances he travels are vast. He cruises at about five miles an hour, though he can make it to twenty for a short time if pushed. If he is lucky his life will continue like this and he will live at least until he is seventy, which is a sperm whale's average lifespan.

For females life is very different. Like African elephants their attachments are strong and their groups matriarchal and supportive. Loyal and united for life, they live and travel in units that number between ten and thirty: mothers, daughters, the daughters' female calves and the young males. There is no shortage of babysitters when mothers head to the depths to feed. But the males remain in their family pods only until they reach puberty, until, like young bull elephants, they feel ready to leave.

Storm's four month old calf Scuba was fathered by Scarface. Storm is forty years old now and Scuba is her fifth calf. Since gestation takes about fifteen months and sperm whale calves are nursed for about three years they give birth usually only every five or six years which makes six calves a good number for a female sperm whale.

Being an experienced mother Storm knows that something is wrong with her daughter who is showing symptoms that are similar to Down's syndrome in humans. It could be that pollutants from chemical industries are the cause. Whenever a whale loses weight, and if their blubber is contaminated with pollutants, then toxins are released into other parts of the body – including a mother's milk. As calves are nursed, and take in the high fat, high calorie milk that is the consistency of cottage cheese, they could be ingesting persistent organic pollutants, otherwise known as POPs. Add to those the toxins in whales' prey and those that are absorbed from the water through their skin, particularly if they swim through oil slicks, and the cocktail of chemical compounds keep mounting up.

But for now the pod seems relaxed. Although they spend much of their time hunting they need to rest. But deep sleep is never an option since breathing is, as it is for all sea mammals, a conscious act, an act that needs planning. To sleep too deeply would be not to breathe.

But they also need to be on guard, for there are other hazards too. Killer whales could be on the look out and they know easy pickings can be found in nursery pods. But it is not always the small and vulnerable calves that orcas are after. Since the smaller size of sperm whale cows compared to the size of bulls is quite exceptional, a pod of killer whales can, if large and intent enough, kill an adult cow. And so when orcas attack a nursery pod the adults surround the calves; facing inwards with flukes outwards and slashing, they make a formidable defence, for just one strike from a fluke could kill an orca.

Another danger for sperm whales is the way they position themselves when they are dozing. Their way of resting is to hang vertically, heads just below the surface. This can be precarious, especially in busy shipping lanes.

It is because of a collision with a ferry that Storm and the others are being so attentive to Omura. She lost her calf when it was clipped and killed by a ship's propeller. Six months later she is still mourning. The whales click to her gently and rub against her sides to comfort her. Her calf would have stayed with her for at least seven years.

Because sperm whales prefer water at least six hundred feet deep and away from continental shelves their range is wide and remote. And since they are top of the food chain and live for such a long time any exposure to toxins is long term. For these reasons they are considered to be markers of ocean health which means that to examine sperm whales is to check the state of the oceans. But there is a problem. Where sperm whales go humans finds it hard to follow. Since more is known about dead whales than living whales, and since those dead whales are only a few of the whole number, supposition - guess work - has to be resorted to. And that raises more questions than answers.

For instance: do sperm whales, like Japan's cetaceans, carry high levels of mercury in their muscles and high levels of PCB in their blubber? Are sperm whales contaminated to the same degree as the Arctic's cetaceans (and also Arctic seals and polar bears) or the apparently doomed orcas of Puget Sound? How are sperm whales faring? What is the state of their health? And how many sperm whales are there? Hundreds of thousands? One million? Two million?

The world's human population is predicted to increase to nine billion by 2050 - two billion more than today's count. Industrial output will increase. And so will the human impact on the whales' world.

2

Incredible Journeys

"Every day is a journey and the journey itself is home"
The Narrow Road to the Deep North Matsuo Basho 17th c
Japanese poet

In the northern hemisphere winter is coming to an end and the migration has begun: the whales are heading north to the Arctic seas where the Earth's oceans merge in the cold waters of the most northern latitudes. These are their summer feeding grounds where they will feed well, putting back the weight they have lost during the last four, five, or even six months - their winter breeding season. For throughout that whole, long mating and calving period, and through the whole of their lengthy migration, they have hardly eaten at all.

As summer begins it's always the young whales and adult males that are the first to head north, back to the polar waters that are rich with krill - tiny shrimp-like crustaceans that are the primary food source of a host of marine animals, including the great whales.

Months of feasting lie ahead. The last to head north are, as always, the cows who have calved this year. When, eventually, their journey ends, these nursing mothers will have the most to gain since whale calves grow at phenomenal rates and their mothers, in providing prodigious quantities of milk, will have lost a great deal of blubber, their vital outer layer that is both insulation and energy reserve.

Meanwhile, in the southern hemisphere, at the opposite end of the world, it is summer that is coming to an end. The southern whales are also beginning to head north. Well fed, and blubber regained, they are leaving the Antarctic waters for their winter breeding grounds, the mid-latitude warmer seas.

Thousands of whales on the move; but, given their fixed routines and the areas they range over, it seems unlikely that the northern and southern whale populations ever meet.

In the lagoons off the Mexican state of Baja California, as summer is coming to an end in the northern hemisphere, the first spouts are a sign that the pregnant humpbacks have begun to arrive at their winter breeding grounds. This is where, in these warmer mid-latitude waters, they will give birth. Their young calves could never survive the cold temperatures of polar waters so the newborns need to grow fast and pile on blubber before winter's end and the next migration. Then they will head north, to spend the summer feeding in cold northern seas that teem with food.

By the time the juveniles and mature bulls arrive the baby spouts are a sign that the first calves have been born; spouts that, for new born whales, need to be blown every two or three minutes. Who fathered which calf will never be known, but many of the males will find a mate during this coming breeding season.

As the testosterone fuelled males begin to arrive the atmosphere changes and the peace of the nursery is disturbed by the vying for female attention. It is now, as the competition begins, that the humpbacks' reputation as the acrobats of the whale world is made clear. Despite their huge size and enormous bulk their aptitude for athletic tricks impresses humans as much as it does their target audience: the receptive, non-nursing, females.

Humphrey is a bruiser of a humpback, about as large as male humpbacks get: forty-eight feet and forty tons. His four-chambered heart weighs as much as three adult humans, and, like all humpbacks, he has forty-five throat grooves and lives up to being called a humpback for the way he arches his back into a hump shape before diving. But what marks him out from all the others is the pattern on the underside of his flukes. They are mostly black save for two large white splodges, one in each outer top corner, for all humpbacks have their own, individual pigment patterns, as well as distinctive marks from old wounds.

Now that he is thirty - and well into middle age since his lifespan is between forty-five and fifty years - he has quite a collection of scars. There are the rake marks made by the teeth of killer whales. Some of his circular scars are where barnacles were once attached. The others were made by cookie cutter sharks, small, one and a half foot long, dogfish sharks that grind out plugs of flesh from prey they cannot swallow whole. But Humphrey's worst disfigurement is a long welt across the tip of his right fluke. It looks as if he must have had a run-in with some fishing gear - and a very lucky escape. Usually when animals as big and strong as whales get tangled in fishing nets, rather than being brought to a standstill, they are doomed to drag them wherever they go. As they swim the fishnet, sometimes several hundred feet of it, trails behind. The drag of the water pulls at the netting and it digs ever deeper into their blubber, sometimes down to the bone. The outcome is often a slow and painful death from infection, starvation and, eventually, drowning. But Humphrey is lucky: for now, all is well.

Although he is not as big as the largest females he is still an impressive size – as are his pectoral fins. At eighteen feet they are nearly one third the length of his body, and outstandingly useful for attention- seeking. When he slaps them down on the water they make quite an impression.

No less impressive is his peduncle throw (the peduncle is where a whale's tail begins and includes the muscles that power the flukes). To begin his throw Humphrey puts his head down and pivots on his eighteen foot fins. Then, with his tail tilted sideways and up out of the water, he smashes them both - peduncle and pectoral fins - onto the surface with awesome force. They land with a terrific, thwacking, wallop. It seems clear that this is sign of aggression and a commanding display of his mighty strength. When he is on top form he can perform an immensely impressive twelve throws in a row.

His lobtailing also makes quite an impact. First he raises his flukes up and out of the water, and then, with tremendous might, smashes them down onto the surface. The resounding smack carries underwater for hundreds of yards and is as good a way as any of drawing attention to himself; and perhaps also serves as a warning to other males to back off. Smashing flippers down hard and fast adds to the effect.

The way he swims on his back with pectorals pointing to the sky is no less dramatic - particularly when pectoral fins are as long as Humphrey's. He makes another of striking spectacle by rolling in spirals.

But perhaps the most dramatic display of all is breaching - when a whale rears up and explodes out of the water. Of all the great whales that leap like in this way humpbacks, right whales and sperm whales are the most sensational. Though others – the finbacks, blues, minkes and grey whales - also breach they seem to lack the enthusiasm of the more spectacular performers.

Since whales usually breach when they are in groups it seems breaching has a lot to do with socialising, and, as in Humphrey's case, making his presence felt. To qualify as a breach at least forty per cent of a whale's body must clear the surface. Less than forty is merely a lunge. It takes a lot of practice to make such a giant leap, and perfecting their breaching technique is one of the many lessons calves are taught by their mothers.

Humphrey begins his breach close to the surface and parallel to it. Then, at about eighteen miles an hour, he drives himself up and – more often than not - ninety percent out of the water. At his best he can jump completely clear of the surface. What other competing male would not be intimidated by a series of leaps that propels forty tons of a muscular rival into the air and who lands on his back - or side - with a crashing smack in jets of glittering spray.

Head lunging is similar to breaching except that it is only the whale's head that erupts out of the water. Head lunges are particularly effective when mouths are filled with water and spat over the heads of competitors.

Pec-slaps are yet another of Humphrey's skills. When pectoral fins weigh tons the sound of them smacking down onto the surface carries a long way under water. But tail slaps can be more dramatic as a humpback's flukes are more powerful than even the largest pectoral fins.

Another attention seeking performance is when he puts his head at an angle and up and out of the water; then, ratcheting up the speed, he creates a large wave, like a boat's bow cutting through the water.

Throwing a huge number of tons around is the name of the game, and for Humphrey his most testing display of vigour is in combat: a contest in which the prize was to mate. But he has to wait for the signal: a female who is slapping the water with her great pectoral fins to show that she is on heat.

When the sign comes, Humphrey is not the only potential suitor. One bull is already in pole position. Cows, especially those with calves, often have an escort - a minder - who stays in the background, and is, usually, male. Although he serves as a defender against a potential attackers his main motivation is to be first in line when the cow is ready to mate. Soon other contenders gather round the ovulating female. Usually there are about six, but sometimes the number of eager suitors can be as high as twelve.

Suddenly, without warning and at full speed, the female takes off. The bulls are immediately after her. Swiping their rivals with their massive flukes; crashing their tens of tons of weight against each other; trumpeting as they come to the surface to breathe, the challengers jostle for position as they charge through the water in the race to catch up with the escort and take his place. But, since whales spend most of their time below the surface, that is where most of the action takes place. In fighting groups great blasts of bubbles are blown; tails are thrashed; heads are butted; and flukes, flippers and chins are used for striking. With so much energy being expended things get heated, heated enough to turn the underside of flukes pink.

But for all the furore it seems the battle for females is more about a display of strength than doing serious harm, even if blood is sometimes drawn, particularly on tubercles - the knobbly bumps on snouts, chins, flippers and dorsal fins - that are a distinguishing feature of humpbacks.

These contests - that can last for hours, even a whole day - are well named as 'heat runs'. Not for nothing have they been described as the greatest courtship battle on Earth.

After hours of competing and all the chasing, ramming and planing over waves - sometimes with ten or more males after one female - only one whale can win. But most will have the battle scars

Only once has the coupling of a pair of humpbacks been witnessed. Five males had been so preoccupied vying for the prize that a smaller whale sneaked passed them, slid in behind the female until their bellies touched. Then the opportunist placed his pectoral fin over the female's flank and for about thirty seconds stroked her gently until, it seemed, the act was done. As they broke apart the female released a burst of bubbles from her mouth as if to signal that copulation was over.

It is said that, in the whale world, large females tend to prefer larger males and that males are less discriminating than females. And rumour has it that since humpbacks have relatively small testes and short penises they are less promiscuous than other great whales. But, like so much about the whales world, a great deal is unknown and many assumptions are made.

But even when humpbacks are not taking part in courtship battles they still throw themselves around in their athletic fashion. It looks likely that leaping out of the water and thrashing down flukes and fins, and twisting and turning and splashing on a sensational scale, is just as much an expression of joie de vivre for males and females alike, though for females the spectacles they perform also serve as a tutorial for their calves.

The nursing humpbacks wisely stay clear of all the jousting, choosing to nurture their young in a more tranquil area, where they can spread out and keep quietly and peacefully to themselves. Hardly at all do they communicate with each other. But the bond with their calves is unwavering and their affection palpable. The proof is the way they touch flippers as they swim together and the soft squeaks and grunts they make as if whispering to each other, perhaps to avoid drawing the attention of killer whales. And they have fun too. Mothers give their babies rides on their backs and allow their calves to wriggle up onto the tip of their heads to they can slide down their backs. This last game must have mutual enjoyment otherwise why would humpbacks have been seen giving similar rides to dolphins.

But males can be peaceful too. When not pumped up in a frenzy over females, or occupied with feeding, they spend a good deal of time milling around close to the surface. Often they relax in such a nonchalant, laid-back fashion that they only need to breathe every thirty minutes rather than their more usual fifteen.

Not only are humpbacks renowned for their athleticism; their 'singing' is also legendary. Although their sounds resemble musical notes it is thought that - since whales have no vocal chords and their mouths don't move when they sing - the sound of their songs must come from their respiratory systems.

Hanging fifty to sixty feet below the surface and almost motionless, with heads down and flukes above their heads, the whales project their harmonies out into the ocean. Some tilt themselves at an angle, others hover vertically, and, with pectoral fins swaying gently backwards and forwards, they intone their unearthly mournful songs. Their melodies vary from a high pitched chirping to a deep resounding base, similar to the sound of foghorns. They click and squeak; make plaintive cries and meows, howls and roars; and low, deep moans and groans - invocations that are immensely elaborate.

When one whale begins a song the others take up the same refrain. Some songs last half an hour; others are repeated for hours and even days, often ending in long finales. Novelty and inventiveness are a fundamental part of the performance, and the songs are ever-changing as old arrangements are abandoned and new ones composed. It is said that of all the calls in the animal kingdom the songs of humpbacks are the most embellished, and that no other animals make sounds that carry so far, or last so long.

Like all whale songs the humpbacks' songs vary with the areas they call home and are, like human languages, completely unalike in different parts of the world. Though females' songs (like those of songbirds) are neither as dominant, or as long or complex as the males. But their incantations, both males' and females', carry through the water over huge distances: the whales' way of letting others know where they are.

In January, when the winter breeding season in the northern hemisphere is coming to an end, Humphrey leaves the Mexican lagoons. Someone has to be the first to leave and this year it is him. He is keen to get back to the summer feeding grounds and it's a long way to go: poleward, to the top of the world, up to the Bering Sea where the north Pacific Ocean ends. Here, between Siberia to the west, Alaska to the east, and fringed to the south by the eleven hundred mile-long Aleutian Island chain, is one of the world's most productive fisheries: eight hundred and eighty-five thousand square miles of sea that is thirteen thousand deep at its deepest point. He will have travelled over three and a half thousand miles, a journey that will have taken him over three months. And in all that time had hardly stopped; only when the rare opportunity arose had he briefly slow down to take in some krill or small schooling fish. But now he had reached the shallower waters of the continental shelf and journey's end. It was time to feed in earnest. And soon the others will join him.

First to arrive are the other males. Then come the non-nursing females and after them the juveniles. The young whales need to feed well as they have a lot of growing to do. They will not reach their full size for about another ten years even though some of them may have produced their own offspring before then. The late-comers are always the new mothers who never head north until their calves have put on a good enough layer of insulating blubber to protect them from the cold polar waters.

By the time the migrating whales arrive some will have lost up to one third of their weight - a loss that is only sustainable on account of their size and the mass of their blubber, their remarkable energy store.

This fatty tissue is very different from the fat of land animals and belongs exclusively to those aquatic mammals - like polar bears, seals, walruses, penguins and whales - that have evolved to survive in polar waters. This vital outer layer is not really fat at all but fibrous, stretchy, connective tissue, full of oil-filled cells and rich in blood vessels. It's extremely thick, immensely insulating and, being rich in proteins and fat, a font of energy - a store to live off during the long winter breeding months. When blubber layers are at their best they account for about a quarter the weight of most whales. The exceptions are the Arctic bowhead whales. Blubber makes up about forty percent of their bodyweight and makes these fifty-five feet, seventy-five ton, Arctic whales the second heaviest of Earth's animals. Only blue whales - at twice that weight - are bigger.

During the long days of the northern summer the whales have little more to do than feed and rest. It's those long summer days that make the Bering Sea such an abundant feeding ground. With sun continuously fuelling photosynthesis, plankton develop in blooms so vast they make the Bering Sea one of the most productive bodies of water on Earth.

There are two hundred thousand species of plankton in the Earth's seas and the part these drifting life-forms play in the oceanic food cycle is vital. Some are plants; some are animals; and some are neither animal nor plant but microscopic organisms that include viruses and bacteria.

The plant kind are single-celled floating vegetation. Called phytoplankton (phyto from the Greek for plant and plankton for wandering) these tiny marine plants drift with the currents and they are prodigious: of all the plant life on Earth plankton are the most abundant.

Zooplankton are the animal form and are made up of a huge variety of tiny drifting organisms such as tiny crustaceans; the larvae of fish, seastars and jellyfish; and tiny radiolaria that are noted for their intricate mineral skeletons.

At the bottom of the food chain they all – the plant plankton, the animal plankton and the other microorganisms that are neither plant nor animal - sustain a wealth of life above. All are critical links in the marine food cycle that a myriad of animals depend on from the diminutive krill, whose main feed is zooplankton, and baleen whales, whose main food is krill.

Barely half an inch long krill are tiny shrimp-like crustaceans that are black-eyed, pink-tinged and transparent enough for their digestive systems to be visible. Although they lack individual bulk - since they weigh just a tiny fraction of an ounce - the swarms they form are massive, and measured by the ton.

There are eighty-five known krill species and their fertility is prodigious. Female krill lay thousands of eggs at a time, usually near the oceans' surface. Over several days the eggs gradually sink to the seafloor to hatch, but as they drift down they are already a food source, another form of zooplankton. About forty per cent of the krill hatchlings stay where they hatched, on the sea bed, to feed on iron-rich, rotting organic matter; the rest swim up to the surface to feed on plankton. Those that escape their great number of predators can live for six years; and some have a lifespan of ten.

The various species of krill thrive in all the world's oceans. Sometimes they form blooms so vast they turn the oceans' surface pink and, when swarms are at their most dense, can be seen from space. They are particularly prolific at the poles where they have a food source other than plankton: ice algae, microscopic plants that live underneath the sea ice. With comb-like 'ice rakes' polar krill scoop the algae into their mouths and in just ten minutes one of these tiny animals can clear one square foot of ice algal growth.

Their weight in the waters around Antarctica alone has been estimated to be six billion tons, and their entire global weight has been calculated to be greater than the collective weight of all of the world's human population. Of all species on Earth these tiny crustaceans are probably the most plentiful. Their existence at the base of the marine food chain is fundamental. Neither the whales nor most of the Arctic's animals could survive without them.

In the Bering Sea, between Alaska and Siberia, the whales are in their tens of thousands. But these numbers are low compared with the time before commercial whaling.

It is not just humpbacks that have come for the feasting. Finbacks, right whales, minkes and sperm whales are here too. But there are no blue whales. Even though blue whales are in all Earth's oceans they never travel to enclosed seas like the Bering, Okhotsk or Mediterranean Seas, or to the Arctic Ocean.

Generally the whales make little social contact with each other, though, when food is particularly plentiful they might get together in quite large groups, usually with their own species. But for the most part they keep themselves to themselves, going about their business which is, mostly, feeding.

Since whales spend about about ninety per cent of their time below the surface they are usually out of sight. But there are, nevertheless, many signs of their presence.

Of all the clues spumes are the most obvious: the tall white silvery spouts that whales blow out when they come to the surface to breathe and which, when the wind is up, lean to windward and show its direction as smoke does on land.

Other giveaways are fluke prints, or 'slick' spots. When whales prepare to dive they raise their flukes - their tail fins -and as they drive them down, water is pushed up to the surface where it forms a huge, smooth, egg-shaped oval: a fluke print.

These telltale markers can stay for quite a while after the whale has gone, usually only disappearing when the waves breaks them up. But not all whales put their flukes up before a dive. The blues, right whales, seis, humpbacks and greys do. But fin and minke whales generally don't. Their slick spots are, instead, long and narrow, and formed by their arching back.

Even more dramatic is when a slick spot appears from underneath the surface. Shortly it is followed by a massive head exploding out of the water. Often the head is accompanied by a stream of bubbles, and then, like a great smooth hill, the whale's back rises above the surface. Water cascades down the whale's sides, at first in an unbroken stream until, like brooks on a mountainside, the flow breaks up into rivulets until they too stop and the animal gleams with wetness. Then the whale blows, and a sound like the exhaust of a steam engine carries far across the water. Where the feeding is good there can be tens of whales all blowing and sending up their spumes at the same time.

Sometimes a head might come out of the water, just as far as the eyes. Like a human treading water, the whale holds their position with pectoral flippers, and might stay like this - ten foot of head vertically upwards - for a good thirty seconds. This is 'spyhopping' and a good tactic for getting a view of anything going on at, or just below, the surface.

Such vigilance is necessary since there is one thing that none of the great whales like to have in their sights: a pod of orcas - killer whales. Orcas range over all the world's oceans and they hunt along the whales' migration routes and in their breeding and feeding grounds. They are renowned for their stealth. Their co-operation is legendary. Their approach is always silent. And no whale is too big to be considered prey. Of the humpbacks sighted off Newfoundland and Labrador one third have scars to prove it – which shows that a run-in with killer whales is not necessarily fatal. But not being fatal does not mean the attack has been unsuccessful. Even chunks and strips torn off a living whale provide a meal.

But when orcas do make a kill, and when prey is as large as a great whale, death can never be quick. A favourite orca ploy is 'attack and retreat', often with tens of killer whales coming in from all angles. The main aim of the marauding pods is to weaken their target. They tear into the flesh to cause as much bleeding as possible or, by chewing at flukes and dorsal fins, cripple their victims, who, unable to swim, drown.

But the whales have defence strategies. Tail cocking - when flukes are poised and ready to swipe – makes even orcas think twice about attacking.   Tail slashing is another and it's particularly effective when whales group together; then, with backs turned on the attacking pod and flukes radiating outwards, they swipe them hard from side to side.

For all they have in common each species of great whale has distinctive characteristics. Blues are the largest: one hundred feet in length; one hundred and fifty tons in weight; the most massive animals that have ever lived. Finbacks are the sleekest; and minkes, at twenty-five feet and ten tons the least big. Seis are the most elusive. Right whales have the largest testicles. Humpbacks are the most athletic and of all animals, have the largest appendages: fifteen foot pectoral flippers; they are also the most likely whales to mix with other whale species. Arctic bowhead whales have the most blubber, the largest mouth and the longest baleens. The other Arctic whales are belugas and narwhals. Of all whales belugas are the most tuneful and narwhals have the longest tooth - a single tusk which, at over nine feet, is about as long as the tusks of an adult African bull elephant.

These are the great baleen whales who filter their food through the hairy fringes attached to flexible baleen bones on their upper jaws. In the nineteenth century, when baleen became a particularly sought-after commodity, these whales had the misfortune to become known as whalebone whales.

The baleen – whalebone - whales share a rarity in the mammal world: females are larger than males. The reason - it has been suggested - is that the females' greater size makes them less likely to be attacked by the great whales' only aquatic predator: killer whales. And, since most great whales rarely eat during their long breeding season, it is supposed that their larger size helps them endure months of fasting, particularly the nursing mothers whose calves make such a great drain on their energy reserves.

Most of these great whales are rorquals – named from Norwegian 'røyrkval' meaning furrow whale. The furrows are the deep grooves that run from the chest to the throat. The number depends on the species. Some have just a few; others up to one hundred. Like the bellows of an accordion these grooves expand to allow mouths of the greatest sizes to have even greater capacities.

It's because of their lack of grooves that two great baleen whales fail to qualify as rorquals: the grey and right whales. Greys have a mere two to five furrows, but right whales have none at all, and nor do the Arctic bowhead whales who are a species of right whale. Grey whales compensate from such a paucity of grooves by sucking in and scooping up their prey. And right whales and bowheads – lacking the grooves that make it possible for their mouths to expand the way the mouths of rorquals do - swim with their mouths wide open, constantly sieving their food, which is, mostly, zooplankton -tiny crustaceans, particularly krill, and fish larvae - through their baleen.

But all the baleen whales have their distinct ways of feeding. Although Humphrey's mouth is big enough to accommodate a tongue the size of a small car, his throat, like all baleen whales, cannot swallow anything much wider than a grapefruit. (Even a one hundred foot blue whale - who is twice Humpfrey's length and whose two hundred tons is four times his weight - has a throat no wider than a beach ball). That means he is only able to swallow fish of modest sizes - small schooling fish like herring, mackerel or sardines - and, of course, copious amounts of krill. For these he generally dives down to between five and seven hundred feet. To begin his dive he lifts his flukes high and then, arching his back, with a few beats of his tail he dives under at a steep angle. For about fifteen minutes, and rarely for more than thirty, at a feeding speed of one to three miles an hour, he scoops up vast shoals of krill, or, maybe, small fish or squid.

But his two other methods gain even greater mouthfuls.

One is lunge-feeding which is something only rorquals do – those baleen, whalebone whales who are distinctive for their throat pleats. It works better if one or two others are involved as it requires circling round a shoal of fish who, in their fear and an attempt to save themselves, press together into an ever tighter group, a compressed, round shoal, a bait ball that might be thirty to sixty feet in diameter. To the whales this is nourishment in bulk: a concentrated food supply.

The whales get in position underneath the tightly packed sphere of fish. Swinging their hugely muscular flukes from side to side they gather momentum. Then, with mouths wide open, and throat pleats expanded like a pelican's beak, they lunge at the dense, vast ball. In no time at all their mouths are full, full of water and schooling fish. But when a rorqual's mouth is at full capacity and their throat pleats are fully expanded, they are no longer their slim, aquadynamic, non-feeding shape. They have become the shape of a tadpole and the drag is immense. Just for a moment, until they empty their mouths of water, they are stopped in their tracks. Then, water expelled, they propel themselves upwards; crash through the ocean's surface; swallow their catch; and then dive down for more. They must waste no time. Bait balls rarely last longer than ten minutes.

In their excitement the whales form ever smaller circles and it doesn't take long for the seabirds to spot the tell-tale signs. As they home in, the air is filled with raucous screeching as the birds hover overhead waiting for the whales to break through the surface. As fish spill out of their mouths the birds take their fill. The seals are here too, after the herring, capelin, krill, squid, or whatever has become the feed of the moment. But this isn't always the way it works. Whales sometimes follow the birds that follow the fish shoals, and then it is they who join the birds in a frenetic bout of feasting.

This is extreme feeding and perfect for animals of great size who need to filter through their baleen one and half tons of krill or small fish every day. In just a few hours of lunge-feeding Humphrey can get enough food to keep him going for a whole day.

His third hunting method is bubble-netting. Co-operation is key and more than three whales are needed; sometimes he joins up with as many as fourteen other humpbacks. Working together, with each whale blowing out a stream of bubbles, they circle around shoals of krill or small fish. Then the whales charge through what has now become a vast bait ball until, with mouths full, they explode out of the surface, expel the water, swallow their catch, and repeat the process.

Next time this group of whales will probably find different company since humpbacks are not big on social allegiances – with the exception of mother and calves, and then only during their calf's first year.

A grey whale bursts out of the water in what looks like an ecstatic breach of joy. Griselda is a North Pacific grey, fifty-two feet and thirty-six tons and, at fifty years old, an old whale now. Although she is one of the smaller baleen whales she is, nevertheless, at forty tons, one of the heaviest animals on Earth: eight times heaver than a rhinoceros.

Griselda comes from the north American side of the Pacific where the grey whale population is classified as 'endangered' and, probably, numbers between fifteen and twenty-four thousand animals. But greys on the Asian, the eastern side of the Pacific are even more endangered. Their population is just about one hundred and their classification is 'critically endangered'. At least that is better than the North Atlantic greys. Whaling did for them and they are 'locally exterminated'.

Like Humphrey Griselda also wintered in Baja and she too headed north. Also northbound were her few remaining counterparts from the Pacific's eastern side whose winter breeding grounds are around South Korea. But their destination, their summer feeding ground, is just fifteen hundred miles away in the Sea of Okhotsk, about half the length of Griselda's journey to the Bering Sea.

Her great jump could have been as much for practical reasons as exuberance, or perhaps the two together, for she has sea lice to dislodge. She has had them since she was a new born, passed on by her mother during birth. The orange patches in the creases of her skin - especially around her mouth, nostrils, eyes and genital folds - are where the lice set up home and feed on the skin.The damaged tissue leaves orange coloured marks that make a distinct contrast to her grey-white colouring. In the warmer waters of the calving grounds she has none of this parasite problem because there topsmelt - silvery fish barely a foot long - feed on both the lice and the dead skin. This routine brings mutual benefit: for the fish the lice and dead tissue make a good source of protein while for Griselda the fishes' feeding keeps her skin smooth, and that's quite a task since grey whales don't have the smoothest of skins. But here, in polar waters, there are no helpful scavengers. Instead she has to dislodge the insects herself either by breaching or rubbing herself along the sea bed where the gritty surface is just right for scouring off lice.

But lice are not the only creature on Griselda's skin. There are also barnacles. These are not molluscs, as is often thought, like snails or mussels, but crustaceans which means they are related to crabs, lobsters and shrimps. Like all crustaceans barnacles are protected by a hard shell – a carapace – that develops around them as they grow which is, in the barnacles' case, up to two and a half inches in diameter.

Of all the great whales, greys are the most barnacled and Griselda certainly has her share. The first generation took hold not long after she was a sixteen foot newborn. By now they have attached themselves by the thousand and their accumulated weight is probably about half a ton. The patterns they form are unique and make her easy to identify. Barnacles can live for years - some for up to ten. The greys get their name from the mottled affect left on the skin when their dead, formerly firmly attached, passengers fall off. But it is not just barnacles that mark Griselda. Like so many great whales she too carries the scars of tooth rakes from her run-in with orcas.

To barnacles a whale is a mobile feeding station. It is thought they attach themselves in the whales' breeding season when barnacles are also breeding and laying eggs by the thousand. When hundreds of whales are relatively close together - in square miles of ocean rather than spread out over thousands - a barnacle larva has no problem finding a likely host. But it does not fix itself indiscriminately. When a larva lands on a whale it walks around until it finds a good spot. Favoured places are the head, fins, back and tail flukes, the places where the supply of plankton will be best. Once the spot is chosen the larva digs in, attaching its prongs in much the same way a plant on land puts down roots. From now on it is fixed for life. As its host swims through the ocean all a barnacle has to do is hold out its feathery, filtering feeding arms and scoop up all the plankton it needs. One filter feeder taking a ride on another.

For these free-riding barnacles life on a whale is a good and safe one, safe from the predators - the starfish, sea worms and fish - that seek out their counterparts who set up home on rocks. But there seem to be advantages to the whales too, at least to the males. For when they are competing for females - butting, ramming and slamming into each other - it could be that the barnacles act as a sort of whale knuckle-duster, a bit of extra clout. But these barnacles, whose home are whales, are not jagged like the ones attached to rocks on the sea shore. Just hard. Their smooth and aquadynamic form is in keeping with their host and their mutual needs: to travel through the ocean with as much ease as possible.

Unlike the other great whales greys are benthivores – that is, they feed on the seafloor, on benthic prey. It's for that reason they like the seabed to be within about two hundred and fifty feet and why Griselda usually feeds quite close to shore.

As she prepares to dive she blows heart-shaped spumes that rise fifteen feet high. Then, flukes up, and with a few mighty strokes, she heads downwards to the seabed. Turning on her right side she pushes her two thousand pound tongue down to the base of her mouth and sucks her food and sediment-laden water into her mouth. As she raises her tongue, the water and sediment are pushed out and her prey - the krill, small fish and amphipods (tiny crustaceans that are similar to sand hoppers) - is trapped in the fringed edges of her baleen. Then she passes her tongue over her baleen plates, and swallows her catch.

Sometimes she prefers to rake through kelp beds rather than the sea floor. There she sucks and sieves crustaceans through her light-coloured, one foot long, baleen that is more worn on the right side than the left. It seems that, like humans who are usually right handed, grey whales also have a tendency to right-sidedness.

By the end of her four to five month feeding season Griselda will have fed on about one hundred and fifty tons of tiny benthic creatures including opossum shrimps, or mysids, that hide under rocks; hooded shrimps, also called cumaceans; woodlouse-like isopods that live in the sediments; and her favourite: amphipods that are, taxonomically, crustaceans even though they have no hard upper shell.

A few miles away, in deeper water, Ellie-Baline, a graceful finback, is slapping the water with her flippers. She is seventy feet long and weighs over seventy tons. But, despite her great size, she is sleek and slender, built like a yacht and faster than a steamship. Even her cruising speed – at fourteen miles an hour – is quick; but when she is pushed she can sprint at thirty-five. Only blue whales are bigger. But no whales are faster.

Like all finbacks Ellie's back and sides are dark grey and her belly white. Her lower jaw is dark on the left and white on the right but, conversely, her tongue is white on the left and dark on the right: an asymmetrical arrangement of colours that is unique in the animal kingdom, for no other animal has markings that are un-matched in this way.

She is one of many as there are more finbacks in the south east Bering Sea than any other type of great whale. You can tell from their dorsal fins that they are rorquals, but the long sharp ridge that shows along their backbones when they dive is more distinctive and gives them their other name: razorback.

Like Griselda, Ellie also has parasites to get rid of. All baleen whales carry an assortment of barnacles on their flukes, heads and fins; some even have them on their baleen, though, since Ellie is a fast swimmer, she has only a few. In any case it's not these that worry her. What she needs to get rid of are tiny parasitic crustaceans - copepods - that burrow into her blubber, feed on her blood and irritate her sensitive skin. She can keep their numbers in check by lobtailing - slapping her tail flukes hard down. But she can do nothing about the fin whale roundworms that live in her gut and can, if infestations really build up, inflame renal arteries and eventually cause kidney failure. But for now she feels well and life is good.

Finback whales like being together. Although Ellie is one of a hundred not far from the Bering Sea's St. Matthew Island, she spends most of her time with six others but with Georgie most of all. They often team up and dive together. Humpbacks and minkes are here too and there is clearly enough food for all comers as there are also seals, sea lions, and walruses as well as a great many sea birds: auklets, cormorants and fulmars; gulls, petrels and shearwaters; and, very occasionally, short-tail albatross and red-legged kittiwake - though both are now rare and the International Union for Conservation of Nature has classified them as 'vulnerable'.

As Ellie and Georgie prepare to dive they blow five to seven quick spouts of warm moist breath, breath that, when the air temperature drops below 5°C, condenses in the cold air. Since Arctic summer temperatures range between minus 10° and plus 10 °C, lower than five degrees is not unusual. When the weather is calm the vapour rises up thin and straight and over twenty feet high. Then, with air replenished and lungs full, they arch their long backs - finbacks rarely lift their flukes before diving - and head down to fifteen hundred feet. Usually their dives last about six minutes but never more than fifteen. Moving at nearly seven miles an hour, with throat pleats expanded, they suck in krill, small schooling fish and squid. When food is plentiful they can take in the two tons they need every day in just three hours.

Sometimes, when their prey is dense, the two whales lunge feed. With flukes pumping they charge at their targeted shoal and round them up until the fish form a tightly packed sphere. With their white-side facing the bait ball, and their mouths expanded to four times their resting size, they take in nearly seventy tons - about their own weight - of fish-filled water. Then, swiping their tongues to expel the water and clear the prey from their baleen plates, they swallow.

There are other whales summering in the Bering Sea, all here for the must-have krill, the small herring, mackerel and other small schooling fish.

The seis are at their northern limit for the south west Bering Sea is as far north as they go. The old whalers named them for the way the whales arrived every year off the north coast of Norway at exactly the same time as the coalfish which in Norwegian are 'seje' (and the British call coley)

Seis are sleek and fast and like to hunt in offshore waters. Gliding through swarms of prey they twist gracefully on their sides as they skim up plankton and krill. Usually they hunt in pods of two to five, but when the feeding is good they get together in bigger groups. Unlike the humpbacks, right and sperm whales, seis only breach occasionally, and then usually at an angle, and nearly always land on their bellies.

Minkes, who are also not particularly keen on breaching, are also here. At twenty-five feet and ten tons, these stocky and well-blubbered whales are, despite their size, the smallest of all the northern baleen whales. All minkes have pale undersides and are either black, brown or dark grey on top, but the northern minkes have a distinctive marking: a diagonal band of white on each flipper.

As a rule minke whales aren't keen on the open ocean; they prefer estuaries, bays and fjords. In the polar regions, unlike the other visiting whales, they enjoy spending time in the ice floes. But being among the pack ice can be perilous, particularly when winter is setting in. They could find themselves trapped in the ice fields and have to spend the winter near a breathing hole.

Minkes swim fast, at sixteen to twenty miles an hour. Usually they prefer to be alone, although occasionally they might join up two or three others. Only when shoals of krill or small fish are particularly plentiful do they gather in larger groups. Then - unusually for baleen whales - they seem to segregate by age and sex. Because their blows are brief and they dive quickly without raising their fluke it would be difficult to spot them - if were not for their one unusual whale trait: they seem not to be able to resist the urge to inspect something novel. And so they swim up to boats without showing any signs of apprehension. But this is usually the only time that it is easy to see them, unless they happen to breaching or spyhopping.

Sperm whales are here too - probably about fifteen thousand - which is a small number compared with the seven hundred and forty thousand that are estimated to be in the North Pacific where they probably outnumber all other types of cetaceans. Their revival from the days of commercial whaling is striking and they seem to have recovered more successfully than any other whale species.

Compared to all the great baleen whales sperm whales are unusual for several reasons. Rather than a baleen, filter feeding system, they have teeth for snatching their prey. And unlike baleen whales- where the opposite is true - sperm whale cows are a great deal smaller than the bulls, sometimes half the weight. The head shape of sperm whales is also unusual. Rather than pointed as the heads of baleen whales are they are cube-shaped.

Although sperm whales aren't the only toothed whales they are by far the largest. Others are the twenty-two species of beaked whales - so-called for their elongated jaws, that are similar to dolphins. Although beaked whales are known as 'toothed' whales they hardly enjoy a profusion of dental features. Usually only the males have teeth, and then just one or two pairs. As beaked whales suck in, rather than grab, their prey, their dental features seem redundant for eating. But when it comes to competition over females it is then they probably come in useful.

Only two other species of toothed whales match a sperm whale's size, Baird's beaked whales (who live in the northern hemisphere) and Arnoux's beaked whales (who live south of the equator). These whales – that are so simolar they may even be the same species - are, at about forty foot and fifteen tons , look like hugely oversized dolphins. Of all whales they are the most mysterious and about them very little is known.

The other so-called toothed whales – like killer whales and pilot whales- are aptly named for being toothed, but not for being whales as they are not taxonomically whales at all, but oceanic dolphins. All the same dolphins and porpoises are all known as toothed whales and together with beaked whales they add up to seventy-three species. Given their huge variation it might seem confusing that that some are called whales at all. But describing them as 'toothed' is not. Dolphins have a great number of sharp conical teeth on both upper and lower jaws - some have as many as one hundred and twenty pairs. And porpoises, whose mouths are shorter than dolphins', have between thirty to sixty pairs of spade-shaped teeth.

But for all their variation toothed whales do have one distinction in common. They all have just one blowhole where baleen whales have two, at the top of their heads.

Other seasonable visitors to the Bering Sea are the rotund, thirty foot, northern bottlenose whales – who as their name implies are beaked whales. Like all beaked whales they like to dive from the steep cliffs of seamounts, and hunt deep down to submarine canyons. But of the twenty-two bottlenose whale species only the northern bottlenose whales behave like dolphins, a characteristic which had disastrous consequences when commercial whaling was at its peak. Being playful, curious and, above all, loyal, the whalers knew they would never abandon an injured or distressed member of their pod. Their solicitude made them an easy catch, a catch that peaked in the1890s and again in the1960s. Needless to say their numbers are now diminished, down to an estimated ten thousand from a pre-whaling population of, perhaps, fifty thousand, Though today they are still at the mercy of whalers as the Faeroese still hunt them.

Other beaked whales who spend the summer in the Bering Sea - but whose whereabouts in the winter are unknown - are Baird's beaked whales. Named after Spencer F Baird, the nineteenth century naturalist, their population is estimated to be around thirty thousand. Forty feet in length and the largest of their species they are also known as the giant bottlenose whale and also, for the number of conical tusks on their upper and lower jaws, the northern four-toothed whale. Like the other beaked whales they too have come to feed on squid and deep-sea fish. Baird's range over deep, off-shore waters on both sides of the northern North Pacific and the Kamchatka, Okhotsk and Bering Seas where they dive deep in their hunt for squid. Although they cover a vast area no-one has any idea of their numbers as they, like all beaked whales - save the unfortunate northern bottlenose - are shy, keep themselves to themselves in small pods, and are rarely seen. They have been hunted for hundreds of years, and the Japanese still hunt them now, off Japan's Pacific coast.

Stejeger's eighteen foot beaked whales are half the size of Baird's. They too have other names: the Bering Sea beaked whale and the sabre-toothed whale, after the males' two, forward pointing, tusk-like teeth that protrude from the lower jaw. Skulls found with healed jaw fractures have been taken to show that the males probably engage in fierce fights.

Others who have migrated to the Bering Sea are the small belugas, small in whale terms that is. These twelve to fourteen foot Arctic toothed whales are striking for their round heads and their whiteness – hence their name; beluga is the Russian word for white. But only the sexually mature are white. Calves are born grey or brown.

Since the Arctic is their home the belugas have journeyed hundreds, rather than thousands, of miles and headed south rather than north. Their purpose is also very different from the other whales. Every year, in July, they moult and shed their thick, snow-white, skin. To accelerate the process and to ease the irritation of their old, loose skin, they set off for river estuaries, often in their thousands. When they arrive they waste no time before they begin to rub and scour themselves on the pebbles and coarse gravel beds whistling with pleasure as they rid themselves of not just their year-old skin, but also a year's build-up of parasites.

Their new skin grows back quickly and then these smallest of all whales resume their hunting. They usually form groups of up to twenty-five, usually in shallow water. Their eclectic diet includes bottom-feeders like octopuses, crabs and shrimps, clams, mussels, snails and sandworms; and they hunt several types of fish including salmon, capelin, cod and herring; but their favourite quarry is squid – a preference that gives them another name: 'squid hounds'. Like all other toothed whales they use their teeth for grasping and tearing rather than chewing.

The heads of all toothed cetaceans contain dome shaped organs known as melons. but the melons of belugas are particularly exaggerated – hence their distinct, round heads. Melons contain air sacs that make clicks - or more exactly vibrations - that bounce back from the world around them: reverberations that tell toothed whales - a classification that includes dolphins and porpoises - precisely what size, shape, bulk and texture the things around them are; where they are; and how far away they are. This is their natural echolocation system, their biosonar, that makes it possible to see with sound. Apart from their size belugas' melons have another unique feature,: they change shape as sounds bounce off the mass of fatty tissue.

Also unlike most other whales belugas (but also the other Arctic whales, the bowheads and narwhals and the much-blubbered right whales) have a ridge on their back rather than a dorsal fin. The lack of a back fin is probably a protection against the cold as any protrusion would be a serious source of heat loss for animals that live amongst the pack ice of Arctic winters.

Yet another difference between belugas and other whales is that they spend much of their time close to the ocean's surface and often wallow in water so shallow it barely covers them.

Even in deeper water they choose to rest on the surface, though to feed they dive six hundred to one thousand feet on dives that usually last about ten minutes. But they can dive deeper and for longer if they need to. Their three foot blows are hardly visible, perhaps because they spend most of their time so close to the air that their blows are too gentle, and too small, to make much of an impact.

Other Arctic residents are the elusive narwhals. 'Nar' means corpse in Old Norse and these whales were named 'corpse whale' for the likeness of their mottled black and white skin to the body of a dead sailor. But their scientific name is less gruesome: monodon monoceros. Monondon means one horn and monoceros refers to their one tooth. The latter part of their name is more accurate as the referred-to horn is really an extended molar. Shaped like a slender spiral the elongated tooth grows to over eight foot (almost half as long as a narwhal's eighteen foot body length) and hence their renown as the unicorns of the sea. But this solitary tooth is the males' only dental attribute, which is more than females have as they have no teeth at all. Nevertheless narwhals are classified as toothed whales and what they lack in quantity they make up for in quality. For centuries the males' horn-like tooth has been highly prized. In the Middle Ages 'unicorn horn' was about ten times more valuable than gold. Today its worth is assessed in feet and the going rate for a narwhal tusk is about US $125 a foot.

What use the narwhals make of their single, eight foot tooth is something of a mystery. Sometimes the males whistle mournfully as they rub their tusks together. It has been suggested that this might be a way of asserting dominance. But it also looks as if their single long tooth could be a sensory organ. Recent research shows that the tooth, having no enamel, is extremely sensitive to changes in the temperature of the water and its salinity. Could it be that the males use these senses to guide their toothless female counterparts on their migration?

Narwhals, like belugas, also head south in summer, but only as far as where the waters are ice free. Even though they are spread out all over the northern polar regions it is rare to see them in the Bering Sea. But wherever they are, they prefer to be far from shore surrounded by thousands of miles of open ocean.

Only when they are migrating do they come in sight of land. Then their timing is so regular that they press on regardless of sea conditions, sending out their echolocating clicks, whistles and squeaks as they travel down the 'leads', the channels of ice free water.

In winter they feed amongst the pack ice. But this is a risky place to be. If there is a sudden change in wind direction or a sudden fall in temperature the ice floes can quickly fuse together. Then the whales, often in their hundreds, become trapped, sometimes fatally if they can't break the ice to make breathing holes. Or, if they get stuck in a relatively small area, they can make easy pickings for polar bears. Belugas often suffer the same fate.

Until the middle of the twentieth century the Innuits of Greenland and Canada relied on narwhals for almost everything they needed: oil, meat, tent poles, sled runners. Nothing was wasted. But the semi-nomadic life of the indigenous Greenlanders and Canadians is coming to an end and rifles are replacing traditional hunting methods. Now narwhals are more likely to be shot than hunted in the traditional method. The whales often sink before they are landed; some escape wounded; and there have even been reports of novice gunmen using the whales for target practice. For the first time it looks as if narwhals are in danger of becoming 'endangered'.

Other permanent Arctic dwellers who visit the Bering Sea are the sixty foot, seventy-five ton bowheads. Depending on the state of the sea ice they usually arrive between the end of November and the middle of December and stay until well into April. Like the belugas and narwhals they too travel southbound down the 'leads'. But in winter, unlike the other Arctic whales, bowheads thrive in areas that are fully covered with sea ice where they use their great heads and huge power to break through the ice to breathe.

Earth's oceans are home to six species of porpoises, thirty-three species of marine dolphins, and four species of river dolphins (who live in the ocean as well as in rivers). At first glance the difference between dolphins and porpoises is not obvious. But on closer inspection dolphins' 'beaks' are more pointed than the blunter snouts of porpoises. And dolphins have conical teeth whereas the teeth of porpoises are spade-shaped. Also dolphins are bigger: about twelve foot compared to a porpoises' average of seven foot, and a size difference that makes it sensible for porpoises to keep out of their way. Humans have witnessed dolphins bullying their smaller fellow marine mammals to the point of killing them, and tossing them around the way cats play with mice.

Dall's porpoises also live only in the northern hemisphere, in the North Pacific, and some spend summer in the Oceans' adjoining seas, the Bering and Okhotsk Seas and the Sea of Japan. They are easy to recognise as their black and white markings are similar to killer whales' although - at little more than six foot long - they are only about a quarter the length of an orca. But they are just as fast and being able to notch up bursts of about thirty-five miles an hour makes them the fastest of all small cetaceans. They normally hunt fifteen hundred feet deep for small fish, like herring and mackerel, and cephalopods, like squid, octopus and cuttlefish. Usually they go round in pods of up to twenty

Although porpoises generally tend not to draw attention to themselves and usually keep well away from boats, But Dall's porpoises are unusual among porpoises: they like to seek out fast ships and bow-ride in front of the fast-moving vessels. But they have another, though pitiable, distinction: currently they are among the most hunted of all cetacean species. The Japanese kill ten to fifteen thousand a year.

It would be easy to assume that in this northern Sea's vast expanse of wilderness, where so many whales come to feed in summer, that there would be food enough for everyone. But half of the US's seafood is caught in the Bering Sea and the Russians fish there too. In the late 1980s, fishing trawlers from Japan, China, Poland and South Korea, together with several other countries, removed millions of tons of pollack. By the early

1990s, the pollack population had crashed and has still not recovered.

Overfishing the pollack is said to be the cause of the eighty per cent fall in Stellar's sea lions and the fifty per cent drop in the numbers of fur seals. Sea bird numbers have also plummeted. According to the RSPB of Scotland since 1996 skuas are down by eighty percent; the Arctic tern population has dropped by seventy-two per cent; and kittiwake numbers have fallen by sixty-eight per cent.

But fishing has done more than take an abundance of pollack. Bottom trawling - which of all fishing methods is the most destructive - has ravaged vast tracts of the shallower continental shelf. This type of trawling scours the sea bed; wipes out entire ecosystems; and leaves swathes of barren waste land in places that once teemed with a huge diversity of life. Recovery is always slow and can take hundreds of years.

But in this remote northern place there is more than overfishing to worry about. Although far removed from any manufacturing, the water is not as pristine as it might seem. Synthetic chemical compounds that are used in a huge number of industries have been carried ever northward by the seasonal patterns of winds and tides, And so, due to the weather and oceanic movements, these toxic pollutants have been found in the Arctic's people, fish and sea mammals. Adult Inuits have been found to have PCB levels seven times higher than the rest of North America's adult population. And where whale meat is sold for food there are warnings of its toxicity.

As autumn approaches the sun's orbit becomes ever lower another annual exodus begins. Soon the ice will begin to form and a great part of the Bering Sea will again freeze over and for six months the sun will not rise above the horizon.

But strange things have been happening to the Bering Sea's winter ice cover. Over the last three decades the Arctic ice has been consistently decreasing. Yet in 2012 the extent of winter sea ice bucked that trend: it covered a far greater area than usual, and melted later than usual. But in February 2018, off Alaska's western coast, the opposite happened. Nearly a third of the sea ice disappeared in just eight days. Not only was the rate of melt unprecedented, but the Bering Sea had the least winter ice in recorded history.(At the same time lower latitudes were experiencing unseasonally late freezing temperatures). It seems winters in this part of the Arctic are not as predictable as they used to be.

Only the hardiest animals remain for the long polar winter: the polar bears, walruses and seals; and, of course, the Arctic whales: the bowheads, narwhals and belugas. The krill will feed off the algae that grows underneath the ice and they will thrive and reproduce. In turn they will be foraged by those higher up the food chain and the virtuous, abundant cycle will continue.

As the whales who have summered in the north head south, the whales in the southern hemisphere are also south bound.

Powered by their massive tail flukes the southern whales are setting out from the southern coasts of Africa and South America, from the coasts of India and Asia, Australia and New Zealand, and all the great expanses in between. They are travelling down the South Pacific, the Indian and South Atlantic Oceans, heading polewards towards the Earth's most southerly waters: the Southern Antarctic Ocean.

The great baleen whales are on their way to the edge of the pack ice: the blues, fins, humpbacks, the southern right whales and the minkes. The seis and Bryde's (pronounced broodus) are also heading south but they will go no further than the sub-Antarctic waters. But there are no greys as there are none south of the Equator. The orcas are also here, the killer whales who are as ubiquitous as humans and with whom we share the distinction of being Earth's most widespread mammal species. They have come to feed on marine animals, especially the Antarctic minkes. who spend much of their time in groups of two to four, feeding at the edge of the ice.

In 1984, south of the Southern Hemisphere's fortieth parallel (40°S), at Earth's most southern point, the International

Whaling Commission (IWC) established the Southern Ocean Whale Sanctuary (and the Commission's second protected area for whales; the first was the Indian Ocean Sanctuary). The area covers twenty million square miles and was intended to be a non-whaling zone. But the Japanese refuse to recognize its legitimacy and continue to hunt there for what they call 'research purposes'. Every year they take several hundred whales, with minkes a favoured target. Despite the numbers killed, minkes are probably still the most numerous of all southern cetaceans. Some researchers calculate their numbers to be in millions, though as always the figures depend on whose counting. And perhaps the point they are trying to prove. For instance the Japanese justify hunting minkes by claiming their population is booming.

Other seasonal visitors include sperm whales who seem to have made as an impressive a comeback in the southern hemisphere as they have in the north despite the extent of their slaughter during the eighteenth, nineteenth and twentieth centuries. It is said that, in the Southern Ocean, two million sperm whales were killed in the twentieth century alone. But only the males are here as females tend to stay in their nursery pods in tropical or subtropical waters, all year round.

But the great whales are not the only cetaceans who have migrated for the seasonal bounty. Bottlenose and hourglass dolphins, spectacled porpoises and long-finned pilot whales are here too. And so are Arnoux's beaked whales who are so similar to the northern bottlenose that they might even be the same species. Being deep divers they, like their northern counterparts, keep close to the steep sides of deep water escarpments and seamounts. As they are rarely seen by humans it is impossible to even guess how many there are.

Most of the animals that have come to the Southern Ocean in summer have come to hunt for krill, squid and fish. And those animals include humans. Although the Southern Ocean is a dangerous and expensive place for commercial fishing the profits can be so great that it makes the danger and expense worthwhile.

But many species are being overfished, like Antarctic rock cod, mackerel icefish and krill – krill for processing into fishmeal to feed farmed animals including farmed fish; for fish bait; and also omega-3 vitamin supplements. So now there are fears of a shortage of even these abundant tiny crustaceans that support the food chains that so many animals including the cetaceans - the whales, dolphins and porpoises - depend on.

There are many claims for the longest migration; not from the whales who seem not especially competitive except when it comes to finding mates, but from those oceanic enthusiasts, marine biologists whose satellite-tags track the whales so exactly.

There were problems with the first tags that often came unattached from the whales' soft skin and blubber. The accoustic signals were no better as they were hampered by noise interference. But that was in the 1970s. Now tags are fixed by barbs like those in fishing hooks and are much more stable and very much lighter. And with transmission by satellite, communication is more reliable too.

These latest tracking devices have made it clear that when whales travel to their breeding or feeding grounds they keep to their usual routes with unremitting accuracy. Bad weather might slow them down, but in spite of currents and tides that could easily push them off course, they invariably keep on track.

The longest journey ever monitored - and probably the longest that any mammal has ever undertaken in the wild - was a female humpback's. She had travelled six thousand, two hundred miles from the reefs off Brazil to Madagascar in the Indian Ocean off Africa's east coast. And once, six adult humpbacks and one calf travelled five thousand, one hundred and sixty miles from Costa Rica to Antarctica. But it seems these journeys were one-offs and no-one can explain why they were made.

But if this is a competition over distance the seis and Bryde's are both out of the running since they never venture further than subpolar waters. And the well-blubbered right whales and minkes find tropical waters too warm, so that cuts their migration distance down too.

As for the other great baleen whales who travel such huge distances on their seasonal migrations, it seems there is not much to choose between them. For instance, those whose journey takes them from the Mexican lagoons to the Bering Sea always travel within sight of the coast and probably notch up between five and six thousand miles - a journey that could be cut down, if the whales chose to travel in a ruler-straight line - to three and half thousand.

But if the competition was for speed the seis might be the likely winners. The tag of a sei killed by whalers showed he was two thousand two hundred miles from where he had been tagged in Antarctic's Southern Ocean ten days before. So when it comes to which of the great baleen whales migrate the greatest distance - the blues, the fins, the humpbacks, seis or greys - it 's a close call.

But how they navigate is still a mystery. Do they follow fish shoals or migrating birds as Herman Melville (author of the whaling novel *Moby Dick*) thought sperm whales did? Or do whales, like birds, have some internal clock? Or is it the water's temperature that guides them along their distinct corridors? Or do they follow the topography of the ocean bed - the ridges, plateaus, reefs and canyons? Or is their migration route marked by the oceans' sounds that they are so attuned to? Or might they navigate in an entirely novel way, unlike any other animal, by a technique yet to be discovered?

Despite the intrusion made by humans, the whales' vast marine world is still a wilderness and all the oceans' animals are wild animals (unless farmed fish – like salmon, sea bass, catfish and cod –are included). On land it's very different. Only four four percent of land mammals are wild, and of those that aren't nearly seventy per cent are farmed and over thirty per cent are humans (who, if calculated by weight, are outweighed by cattle by half as much again). For birds the ratio is thirty per cent wild and seventy per cent farmed.

But as humans, cattle and other farmed animals increase the number of wild animals decrease as their environments become ever more confined. But in the oceans there are boundless places where the whales can disappear from human tracking; and many routes and destinations that remain out of limits to even the most sophisticated marine technology. So perhaps we shouldn't be surprised that ninety-five per cent of this immense marine world - that covers seventy-one percent of Earth's surface - is unexplored, and possibly two thirds of its species still unknown. Most are expected to be crustaceans and molluscs but it's likely, according to some marine biologists, that there could be eight species of cetaceans not yet identified.

But what does 'explored' mean? Mapping, obviously, but in what detail? Small scale - a large area depicted in a small space? Or large scale – covering a small area in much detail? And what about cataloguing the incalculable number of undiscovered organisms that are down in the unknown, and inaccessible, ocean depths?

In 2015 nearly fifteen hundred new sea creatures were identified including sponges, jellyfish and an Australian humpback dolphin. And in the Amazon rainforest – which at least is humans' natural element - tens of new species are discovered every year: monkeys, snakes, frogs, parrots and also, in 2014, in the Brazilian rainforest, a pink river dolphin.

It seems a very great number of Earth's mysteries are yet to be solved. But one thing is clear. As the human population increases the changes we are making to the whales' world are intensifying.

3

Oil Wells That Swim

"The gunners themselves admit that if whales could scream, the industry would stop for nobody would be able to stand it."
Harry Lillie, ships doctor on the *Southern Harvester,* 1946

For thousands of years sea faring people all over the world hunted whales, mainly for their meat. But when it was found that sizeable profits could be made from rendering whale blubber into oil for lighting, the whale trade developed apace. And so, at the beginning of the seventeenth century, whale oil became the first commercially important oil and a must-have commodity.

From then on factories, shops, lighthouses, private houses, public houses, offices, businesses and streets began to be lit by a whale-based lighting system. By1750 London was considered the best lit city in the world - lit by the oil rendered from the blubber of the great whales. And when, from the late 1700s, whale oil lamps were used to light the wool and cotton mills work could carry on well into, and even throughout, the night.

When machines began to replace hand labour whale oil was more in demand than ever. It became necessary for greasing the wheels and cogs of the Industrial Revolution. But there was more to be had from whales than oil for lighting and lubrication for machinery. Technical innovation developed apace and soon the raw materials of almost every industry included whale parts. And consumerism grew as it never had before.

Whale bone (the strong, flexible baleen plates that filter the food of baleen whales) was used for springs in horse-drawn carriages, typewriters and watches. It was made into frames for travelling bags and trunks; into ribs for umbrellas and parasols;

and for riding crops and buggy whips. It was used in hoops for skirts and supports in corsets and for shaping women's hats. It was made into collar stiffeners, cuff-links, shoe-horns, fishing rods and medical trusses.

From whale 'ivory' (the teeth of sperm whales) piano keys, chess pieces, mah-jong counters and dominoes were fashioned. And so were walking stick handles, boxes, toys and food choppers; watch stands and rulers; cigarette holders and pipes; and buttons, ear-rings and broaches.

Out of whales' tendons shoe laces, tennis racket strings and surgical sutures were made.

Skeletal bones were used as building materials and cattle fences, and to make kitchen utensils and knitting needles.

Ambergris (the secretion that aids the expulsion of squid beaks from the intestines of sperm whales) became a fixative for perfume and the Anointing Oil in coronation ceremonies.

Eventually whales, who for centuries had been regarded as the raw material for a plethora of products, became less desirable. In the 1860s, kerosene began to replace whale oil for lighting and the demand for whale oil fell. Baleen also began to be replaced by other materials such as gutta-percha, a rigid natural latex. In 1838 Charles Goodyear, an American chemist, heated rubber mixed with sulfur and linseed oil and invented Ebonite. In 1907 Belgian chemist Leo Baekeland invented the first entirely synthetic plastic: Bakelite. And a replacement for baleen was born. The 1920s saw PVC (polyvinyl chloride) produced commercially for the first time. And in 1957 polypropylene began to be used in packaging and many other everyday items.

But when the first world war broke out whale oil, once again, became the priority. It was the cheapest source of glycerine for processing into nitroglycerin for making explosives, cheaper than vegetable oils or the fat of farm animals. It also made a good lubricant for guns. And soldiers at the front used a salve made from whale oil to protect them against trench foot (a battalion of about a thousand soldiers used about ten gallons every day). For the Norwegian and British whalers, who were hunting whales in the Antarctic, business was good again.

Although the supply of whale oil had peaked in 1845 and whale oil had been replaced by gas and electricity for lighting, it continued to be in demand for another hundred years. Until the 1950s it was the main ingredient in cooking-fat, margarine and gelatine. It was used in lipstick, skin cleansers and skin cream; in soap, varnish and paint; in polish for shoes and tanning oil for leather. It was in anti-freeze, car-wax and in engineering coolants. Parchments, printing inks, artists' pigments, wax crayons, linoleum and oil-cloth all contained whale oil. From the livers and glands of whalesthe pharmaceutical industries extracted liver-oil, iodine, hormones, vitamins and insulin. And the chemical industries processed whales' skeletal bones for calcium for fertilisers.

Ever since the first whalers drove small whales into coves, as the Faroe Islanders, Greenlanders and Japan's Taji dolphin hunters still do today, whaling has became ever more efficient - and more deadly.

In the seventeenth century, when the first industrial whaling fleets set out in search of whales to render into oil for lighting, the number of ships was few, but it quickly grew. But as the number of whaling ships increased the number of whales decreased and the whalers had to go to further off-shore to find them.

By the time Moby Dick was published in 1851 hundreds of whaling ships were hunting whales all over the world, thousands of miles from their home ports. Most stayed at sea for several years, and when those that were far from land had to process their quarry on board, they became in effect, floating factories.

Those early ships – that were powered by sail and whose 'catcher boats' were rowed by the crew – were no match for the speed of the fast blue and finback whales. Instead the whalers had to settle for slower whales such as right whales, so-called because they were considered the 'right' whales to catch.

There were many reasons that made right whales right. At forty feet and seventy tons they are big. They feed near the surface and close to shore. They are slow, and, with a top speed of just ten miles an hour, the slowest of all the great whales. Their one foot thick blubber not only yielded massive amounts of oil, its other advantage was buoyancy. Dead right whales float, and a floating whale is relatively easy to tow to base for processing. But best of all is the right whales' calm nature. They were seldom alarmed, even by unfamiliar boats, which made killing right whales considerably less perilous than hunting more lively whales. Although the quality of their oil was poor – it was thick, brown and smelt of fish - their baleen made them profitable.

Bowhead whales are closely related to right whales and they were attractive to whalers for the same reasons, except for one thing. Bowheads are Arctic whales who never leave the cold polar seas. But the risks of whaling in the pack ice were made worthwhile. With blubber one and half foot thick, the thickest of all whales', and baleen plates fourteen feet long, the longest of all whales' – bowhead whales were hugely profitable.

Least favoured by the whalers were humpbacks. They sank after killing, their baleen is not premium quality and the older the whale, the darker and less profitable the oil. Nevertheless a second-rate, stinking, forty ton whale was better than no whale.

But there were other whales in the nineteenth century whalers' sights: the sperm and grey whales. Like humpbacks the greys were not ideal either. Their dark oil was poor quality and their baleen was neither plentiful – being just eighteen inches long - nor of premium quality. Worse still, grey whales are aggressive. What made them particularly feared – and the reason the whalers called them 'devil fish' - was that they sometimes attacked the small 'catcher boats'. But these whales were plentiful. No sooner had it been discovered that they could be found in large numbers in their calving lagoons than the hunt was on. They were hunted to near extinction.

In calm weather a whale's spout can be spotted as far away as eight miles. The moment the lookout, up high on a masthead, sent out the cry "There she blows" all hands rushed on deck and the catcher boats were lowered: two or three boats each crewed by five to ten men. The hunt was on.

The crews rowed to where they expected the whale would come up to blow. As whales have acute hearing the men had to wait as quietly as they could, particularly if they were hunting sperm whales, humpbacks or greys who, unlike docile right and bowhead whales, swim away from unusual sounds.

If the crew's estimation was right the whale would surface close enough for the harpooner to lodge two harpoons (fixed to a single tow-line) into the whale's blubber. If the throw was hard enough and the barbs dug in they could cause a mortal wound. But death was never instant. The shock of the attack would make the whale take off on a 'run' that could last for hours. As the whale attempted to escape it was crucial to let out enough rope: too little and the boat could be pulled under when the whale dived. Known as the 'Nantucket sleigh ride' - in the nineteenth century Nantucket was then the capital of US whaling - the open boat could be dragged for hours over waves that were sometimes streaked with blood. The pace was fast, particularly if the whale was a sperm whale; they can keep up a speed of about twenty-five miles an hour, at least for the first hour.

But there was no guarantee of success. This was a matter of life and death - and not just the life or death of the panicking animal. Sometimes the whale broke free. Sometimes the boats capsized in rough seas. Sometimes boats were overturned by the whale. And sometimes men would be thrown out by the pitching of their boat as the macabre 'sleigh ride' went on its way.

If the whale failed to escape the defeated animal would eventually be overcome with exhaustion and give up the fight. At that point the whalers pulled in the line and closed in for the kill. The harpooner and 'boatheader' (who was in charge of the steering) changed places - a hazardous thing to do in choppy seas. The harpooner then plunged a lance into the whale's heart or lungs and the dying animal would swim violently in ever smaller circles until, finally, they gave the water one last beat with their tail '. The end was often marked by a final spout of thick blood before the whale rolled over on their side - the final action of a death throe that was called a 'flurry

Once the whale was dead no time was wasted. Immediately, a hole was cut in one of their flukes, a tow rope was tied through the hole, and the corpse - that might weigh fifty tons or more - was towed to base for processing. Only if the whalers were close enough to a whaling station could they land their catch on dry land. And only if the winds were favourable could the whale ship come to the whalers. Often the crew had to tow their catch back to the ship. For those far from land this was often a race against sharks. If the voracious fish appeared in large numbers, which was likely in the Pacific, they could cause a great deal of damage to a hard won carcase in a surprisingly quick time.

As soon as the whale was lashed to the ship's side the crew divided into two hour shifts and the processing began. First the blubber - called the 'blanket' - had to be 'flensed'. Using a winch, the animal's outer layer was peeled off in a method similar to removing the skin off a piece of fruit. At the same time other members of the crew would be hard at work trying to interrupt the sharks' feeding frenzy by jabbing at the feeding fish with 'cutting tools'. As they skidded on the back of the oily corpse each man was kept reasonably safe by a rope attached to a crew member on deck. Meanwhile other deck hands, using blubber-spades, would be cut the blubber into manageable pieces - 'blanket pieces'- for throwing into the blubber room.

Eventually, when the whale had been stripped of all that was wanted its remains were sent back to the sea, and the sharks could feast without interference. Then the fires underneath the 'try pots' - huge iron pots built into the deck on brick bases - were lit, the blubber was thrown in, and 'boiling out the oil' began. Finally, after cooling, it was put into casks that were placed in the hold for storage. This rendering process was time consuming and could take weeks.

Of all the whales the biggest prize was a sperm whale, sometimes called a cachalot from the Portuguese for 'big head'. And it was the head that yielded the greatest reward. Even though female sperm whales might be half the weight of a right or bowhead whale it was quality, not quantity, that made the rewards so great: there was no other oil that was as pure as sperm whale oil. Because it burnt bright and clear, and without smoke or smell, it was in great demand for both domestic and public lighting. And, since the oil remained fluid regardless of temperature, it was by far the best oil for lubricating the new-fangled machines of the Industrial Revolution. Sperm whale oil was the luxury oil; the oil that was the most expensive and the most valued.

The first stage in processing a dead sperm whale was removing the spermaceti, which, chemically, is liquid wax, not oil, and so-called from the Greek for seed 'sperma', (because originally the liquid was mistaken for the whale's semen) and 'ceti' meaning whale.

To the whale the spermaceti organ is vital for sending and receiving their biosonar signals, and also serves as a buoyancy device. But for the whalers this was the most profitable part of their booty. If a whale was fully grown, one head, a head that is one third of the whales entire length, could yield three to four tons of the 'liquid gold'. On no head has a greater price being put.

But butchering a sperm whale was considerably more complicated than 'cutting into' a baleen whale.

First the head had to be severed from the rest of the body - a huge undertaking given that a sperm whale has no discernible neck. Next, like lifting the lid of an immense treasure chest, the top was opened up, buckets were dipped into the vast cavity, and the yellow spermaceti bailed out.

Next the orange 'junk' was taken from the lower half of the forehead. A 2016 study suggests this fatty structure might be designed for ramming, for smashing either other males - or whaling ships. Given the aggression of sperm whales this seems a plausible explanation, and the discovered remains of sunken whaling ships seem to support this theory. But junk seems an inadequate description since this wax, although not as pure as spermaceti, is superior to blubber and so more profitable. And even a sperm whales' blubber was considered superior to the blubber of other whales.

Finally the lower jaw was severed and the teeth removed. Although sperm whales' upper jaws are toothless they are not redundant: they house sockets that accommodate the teeth in the lower jaw. When a single tooth is eight inches long and weighs a couple of pounds - and some sperm whales had up to twenty-six pairs - these too were a profitable commodity. They also made good material for the whalers' artwork, their scrimshaw. It could be months before the next whale was sighted and carving and etching whaling themes on whale ivory helped pass the time.

After the head had been processed and the blubber flensed there was still more treasure to search for. On very rare occasions a sperm whale's intestines could yield a bounty even more valuable than gold: ambergris – the waxy, flammable, faecal-smelling excretion which eases the passage of squid beaks from the stomach of sperm whales. But ambergris becomes sweet smelling with age – hence its most notable use as a fixative for perfumes. It was also once highly valued as an aphrodisiac; a food additive; as incense in religious services; in medicine; and as a status symbol.

Though to find any ambergris at all was extremely unusual - it's said that it's produced in only one per cent of sperm whales. But there was always the chance of a lump weighing as much as one hundred and fifty pounds, a find worth considerably more than its weight in gold. In the 1850s an ounce of gold was worth US$21. An ounce of ambergris could fetch US$40.

Such a find meant riches for all hands, for the ships' profits were shared between the owners and the crew. The owners took between sixty and seventy per cent and the balance was apportioned to the crew by rank, down to the very lowest.

As whales became scarcer prices went up and whalers were forced to go after smaller whales further from home. The rewards were always hard won - or might not be won at all. Some ships returned empty and some were wrecked with all hands lost.

Nevertheless, despite the immense dangers involved in the chase, the value of the oil made the formidable risks worth while, including processing a whale into its lucrative parts which was hardly less hazardous than the perilous quest. Working on decks smeared with blood and oil and as slippery as an ice rink; using cutting tools sharp enough to slice through limbs; cutting strips of blubber heavy enough to crush a man; with sharks below; in rough seas; up close to vats of scalding oil; in wooden ships with furnaces raging under the try pots - rarely did a whale ship return with its full complement of crew. But if, barring a profusion of likely misfortunes, the ship returned to port the risks paid handsomely - especially if the hold held casks of sperm whale oil.

The heyday of whaling was between the1820s and the1860s. In those days the Americans, British, Dutch, French, Greenlanders, Icelanders, Norwegians and Japanese were all after the same quarry. But it was the Americans who dominated this global industry.

By the1860s, when oil wells began to be drilled and petroleum – crude oil - began to be extracted, the demand for whale oil fell and the age of the great American whalers began to come to an end. But it was not the end of whaling. New ways to kill whales were invented and the new inventions upped the ante. As whale grenades and exploding harpoon guns replaced hand-thrown harpoons whaling methods became ever more efficient and the industry developed apace.

The first explosive harpoon was designed to slow the whale down. It came on the market in 1863. After that came the bomb lance. This weapon exploded deep in the whales' body and was much more effective and fewer whales escaped. Today's weapon of choice is the Hvalgranat-99 (or whalegrenade-99) which is used by the Norwegians, Icelanders, Greenlanders and Japanese.

Ships also became faster and as soon as they were powered with steam could outrun the biggest and fastest whales: the blues, the Bryde's, fins, humpbacks and seis. Ships also became larger. Now hunting, killing, processing, storing and preserving, could be carried out on board on an even greater scale. The new custom-built factory ships became hugely efficient. The first was the wooden steam shipTelegraf. She sailed out of Spitzbergen in 1903. After several months at sea she returned to Sandefjord with 1,960 barrels of oil from fifty-seven whales, forty-two of whom were blue whales.

In the following forty years more whales were killed than had been killed in the previous four hundred.

When, in 1925 the Norwegians, invented rear slipways whaling became more efficient still. Whales could be now be winched onto the main deck and whalers no longer had to work on whales lashed to ships' sides. By the 1950s the largest whaling ships were the size of aircraft carriers and their crews numbered several hundred. Their effectiveness was ruthless. Technological advantages reduced the risk to the whalers and upped the death count of their quarry.

Pods were tracked by aeroplanes and helicopters. No sooner were whales sighted than up to twelve catcher boats were after them. And no sooner had the whaleboats made their kill than the crew of the 'buoy boats' immediately took over, pumping air into the dead whales until they floated to make it easier to tow the quarry to the factory ship for butchering, and freeing the catcher boats to head off to kill more whales.

In the1950's it was Britain and Norway who dominated the whale trade, killing, mostly, blues and finbacks . During the1950s and 1960s their factory ships were 'harvesting' fifty thousand whales a year. The British hoped that whale meat would fill the gap made by the post war food shortage. It was sold as 'whacon' and described as similar to corn beef, but even though it was unrationed it never became popular. Instead whale meat was made into pet food, fish bait, cattle meal and feed for animals in fur farms. But whale oil for margarine remained much in demand.

This was the last big push in commercial whaling. It had begun in 1925, the year that rear slipways were first used, and continued until 1975. In those fifty years commercial whalers killed one and half million whales. The global peak was said to be 1961 though the Japanese reported a record catch between 1964 and 1965. The IWC has calculated that in the twentieth century a total of three million whales were killed, over half of which were fin and sperm whales.

Today just one whaler factory ship remains: the flagship of the seven vessel Japanese whaling fleet, the MV Nisshin Maru.

In 1946, after it had taken five hours and nine harpoons to kill a whale, Harry Lillie, a doctor on the whale factory ship Southern Harvester, said "The gunners themselves admit that if whales could scream, the industry would stop for nobody would be able to stand it".

But a vocal sign of suffering did not seem to have put the old whalers off hunting seis who, they said, made a greeting noise when they came up to whaling boats and a crying sound when they were killed. In fact the whalers were well aware that the cries of an injured whale would lure others to its rescue and they made no hesitation in taking advantage of other whales' seemingly selfless acts.

For all the improvements in whaling technology the degree of the whales' suffering seems not to have lessened at all. Modern harpoons are designed to penetrate about a foot into the whales' blubber. The theory is that shortly after the harpoon explodes the whale is killed by shock waves. If the first harpoon fails then a second is despatched. Whalers claim the average time it takes a whale to die is two minutes.

However the gap between theory and practice can be great. Some whales escape wounded. Some are chased to the point of exhaustion. Or they might be dragged for hours until eventually they drown. And sometimes a whales are still alive when they are dragged up the rear slipway. In that case they are speared or shot again to finish them off.

But there is much about the physiology of whales that is not understood. For instance, the way whales slow their breathing and heart rates (as they do when they dive) makes it difficult to tell when a whale is dead. Could the whale that is lying on the slipway have shut down its vital organs in an attempt to save itself and therefore be in a fully conscious state?

What is clear is that whales have complex social lives and far reaching communication systems. When members of a pod are killed how many in that unit are left bereft? Do other whales know what is happening when others are being chased and killed? Do dying whales send messages far out into ocean for other whales to hear?

Since the 1970s most nations have given up hunting whales - but not all. In 1982 the IWC - who are responsible for setting whale catch limits - put a moratorium on commercial whaling. But the Japanese, Norwegians and Icelanders disregarded the ban and assigned their own quotas. And so the Japanese still hunt Bryde's whales and also fin, humpback, sei, sperm and minke whales. The Icelanders hunt finbacks and minkes. And the Norwegians hunt minkes.

The Japanese claim they hunt whales for scientific research and also to satisfy their market for whale products, especially meat. Since they eat not more than five thousand tons of whale meat a year but six hundred million tons of sea food, whale meat seems a small proportion and not, as they claim, a thriving market.

But the IWC recognise that whale meat is, as it always has been, the main source of food for some indigenous groups. And so the native Alaskans have been granted a permit that allows them to take seventy-five bowheads a year. The Chukotkans of eastern Siberia, in Russia, have permission to hunt a maximum of one hundred and forty grey whales. In the Caribbean the islanders of Grenada, Dominica and Saint Lucia are permitted to hunt short-finned pilot whales, pygmy killer whales and spinner dolphins; and in Bequia, the second largest Grenadine island, where hunting humpbacks has become a spectator sport, the IWC permits four humpback whales a year to be killed.

Although whale-bone and whale oil are no longer in demand new whale products are being devised. High on the list are dietary and pharmaceutical supplements The Norwegians already export dietary supplements based on seal oil to more than ninety countries and they are hoping to have a similar outlet for whale oil. They are currently conducting clinical trials on the effects of whale oil on a range of diseases including heart disease. Their research findings show that no other Omega 3 oils is more effective for treating Rheumatoid Arthritis than whale oil – and this they hope will make killing whales acceptable. But their ambition to add whale oil to the fishmeal they export as feed for farm animals, including farmed fish, seems to rest on a weaker case.

The Icelanders are also hoping to sell whale oil as feed for livestock and farmed fish (rumour has it that they may already do so). Another innovation is whale oil as fuel. The whaling ships of the Icelandic company Hvalur HF are powered by twenty per cent whale oil and eighty per cent diesel, or in other words: fuel that is one-fifth renewable and four-fifths non-renewable. Though, in view of what is happening to the oceans, whale oil, like non-renewable fossil fuels, could also run out.

In 1620 when the first Pilgrims first arrived on the east coast of America they were amazed at the number of whales along the coast of what became known as New England. We can never know what their numbers were then, and neither are we sure how many whales exist today. But estimates have been made.

The US's National Oceanic and Atmospheric Administration (NOAA) has reckoned that before whaling began in earnest the world's humpback population was around one hundred and twenty-five thousand. What is certain is that by the time commercial whaling was banned in 1986 (by the IWC) humpbacks were close to extinction. But their number today, by NOAA's reckoning, is about eighty-five thousand - a remarkable comeback from having been just about wiped out. But there are fourteen humpback populations and some have fared better than others.

The humpbacks who regularly visit Australia's Queensland coast seem to be making the most successful recovery. In 2015 their estimated count was twenty-four and a half thousand and it looks as if they are increasing at about ten per cent a year. Quite a recovery, considering that in the1950s, in all of the Southern Hemisphere, they totalled just a few hundred.

But for the Arabian Sea humpbacks, whose entire population is just about four hundred, it's a very different story. Their territory, in the north western part of the Indian Ocean, has become the principal sea route between Europe and India and now contains some of the world's busiest shipping lanes. From the seven Arab states that border the Gulf of Arabia immense oil tankers carry oil to Europe, East Asia and to North and South America. And from the Suez Canal cargo ships of vast tonnage, loaded with all manner of freight including grain, ores and metals, travel this route on their way to South and East Asia.

But it is not just the oil tankers and bulk carriers that the whales have to contend with. There are also container ships, international cruise ships, domestic ferries, fishing boats, pleasure boats and even warships that sometimes come from various countries to take part in naval exercises. Collisions with shipping are just one of the many hazards these rare humpbacks have to face. They also have to vie with the impacts of gas and oil exploration, the incessant noise of shipping and possible entanglement in fishing gear. To make matters worse these Arabian Sea whales are unique among humpbacks. Usually humpbacks are, of all the world's mammals, the most travelled, but these whales at the northern end of the Indian Ocean never migrate, but stay in these congested waters all year round, breeding and feeding there. No wonder they have been called the world's most isolated whale population. That many suffer from liver abnormalities and skin diseases is a sign that all is not well with them. It looks as if the impacts of mankind's technological lifestyle have weakened their immune systems.

These waters are where, in 1979, the IWC established its first protected area: the Indian Ocean Whale Sanctuary. It covers the whole of the Indian Ocean south to 55°S, including the Arabian Sea. Although Arabian Sea humpbacks are protected from commercial whaling the Sanctuary cannot protect this subpopulation from the busy shipping lanes, or all the other hazards that are the consequences of the industrialisation of Earth's seas.

It's no surprise that the Arabian Sea humpbacks are classified as 'endangered' (under the US's Endangered Species Act that came into being in 1973)which means they are at risk of extinction. So too are the humpbacks in the Western North Pacific; those off Northwest Africa's Cape Verde Islands; the four hundred off the coast of Central America; while the three thousand, four hundred humpbacks that breed off Mexico and migrate to feeding grounds off the Californian coast are listed as 'threatened', which means they are at risk of becoming 'endangered'.

But nine of the fourteen humpback populations a re now off the endangered list. Nevertheless theirs is not a risk-free world. Like their counterparts everywhere, they too have to contend with busy shipping lanes and the possibility of ship strikes and entanglement – the two most common hazards for all cetaceans.

But being on the endangered list it is not the case for minke whales, who are the most numerous of all the great whales. There are almost certainly well over one hundred thousand North Atlantic minkes who, although they are not classified as 'threatened' are threatened by the Icelanders and Norwegians who still hunt them.

The Antarctic minkes, who are slightly larger than their northern counterparts, are thriving too. Also known as southern minkes they are spread out all over the southern hemisphere, over the south Atlantic, the east Pacific and the Southern Ocean.

Estimations for their numbers vary from half a million to over a million.

Once the North Atlantic right whales were also in large numbers - those whales that had been the 'right' whales to catch and whom the whalers found such easy targets. In 1611when whaling began off Svalbard (a cluster of islands between Norway and Greenland) the seas were so full of whales that a captain reported the ships had to pick their way through them. But by the end of the eighteenth century these right whales had all but been wiped out and now, of all the great whales, they are among the most endangered. Their numbers are down to about three hundred, or perhaps three hundred and fifty, and they are showing little, if any, signs of recovery. With their risk of extinction extremely high they join the list of the thirty-one marine mammals that are classified as "endangered" or "threatened."

The plight of the north Pacific right whales, who were also once in great numbers, is even worse. There are just thirty left - eight females and twenty-two males - which makes them the world's smallest whale population.

But the southern right whales seem to be recovering, albeit slowly. The most recent estimates (based on data collected over one hundred and twenty years by the IWC) predict that if these whales continue to recover at the rate they are recovering now, by the beginning of the twenty-second century they will be back to half their pre-whaling numbers. Some are doing well. Those off the South African, Australian and the Argentinian and Brazilian coasts of South America are increasing by seven or eight per cent a year. Nevertheless they are still classified as 'endangered' by conservation bodies in Australia, New Zealand and Brazil. But the number of right whales off South America's west coast, off Chile and Peru, is down to just fifty whales, which makes them 'critically endangered'.

Bowhead whales have been known by many names: Russian, Polar and Arctic whales; and - on account of their high heads - Steeple-tops. Also - for being easy targets - Greenland right whales. As most of these names suggest the Arctic is their home and their conservation status varies depending on which part of the northern polar region they live. Most populations seem to be on the road to recovery, though those in the Okhotsk Sea and off Spitsbergen remain on the endangered list. The data shows that there are probably about ten thousand bowheads living today - down from the fifty thousand that probably existed in the seventeenth century, before commercial whaling began to gather pace.

There have only ever been three populations of grey whales who, like bowheads, all live in the northern hemisphere, but unlike the polar whales, re only fair weather visitors to the Arctic where they come to feed in summer. The North Pacific grey whales are another success story. Also known as California Grays they are thought to number eighteen thousand which NOAA consider an "optimum sustainable population" and so were removed from the endangered list in 1993. But they have some way to go before they are back to their pre-whaling numbers of about one hundred thousand. The story is not the same for the greys of the western Pacific. Their number is down to just one hundred and thirty, which makes them 'critically endangered' and in grave risk of extinction. Worse still is the plight of the North Atlantic greys. Whaling finished them off and they no longer exist.

Blue whales in the Antarctic almost met the same fate. Over nearly seventy years, between 1904 and 1967, more than three hundred and fifty thousand were killed. Only one per cent of their original number - just a few hundred – survived. It was only after the IWC banned their hunting in 1967 that the blue whales in the southern hemisphere had any hope of recovery. Now it's thought their numbers up to two thousand: a comeback from the brink of extinction. All being well, some marine biologists expect that (like the southern right whales) these southern blue whales could be back to half their pre-whaling numbers of, perhaps, one hundred and seventy five thousand,, by 2200. Meanwhile estimations for the worldwide number of blue whales living today vary from between ten thousand and twenty five thousand.

But in the northern hemisphere - where blue whales are not quite as large as their southern counterparts - there is only one success story: the California blue whales seems to have recovered and are now only just three per cent below their pre-whaling numbers of, perhaps, two thousand two hundred.

But the North Pacific blues, whose count is about two and half thousand, are still only half their original number. And the number of North Atlantic blues (according to NOAA's estimations) are probably about one third down, from about one thousand three hundred to five hundred.

Finback whales have fared no better. Between 1904 and 1979 about seven hundred and fifty thousand were killed - and half of those in the1950s – so that now fin whale sightings in the southern hemisphere are extremely rare. But in the North Atlantic it is said their numbers - at forty-six thousand – are good, though whether back to those of pre-whaling days is not certain.

Sperm whales range over all the oceans but their population count is not certain either. Estimates vary from between two hundred thousand to a million, and since some reckonings put their numbers at two thirds of what they were in pre-whaling days they are listed as vulnerable. But other toothed whales, like killer whales, whose global population is calculated to be at least half a million, and pilot whales, who are thought to number one million, are not considered endangered. And neither are they officially whales but - taxonomically - oceanic dolphins.

The number of seis, those sleek, lean, speedy whales – and the third largest baleen whales after blues and finbacks - is between forty thousand and sixty thousand. Being less blubbered and less profitable they only become a target for whalers when the stocks of blue and fin whales began to run low. But there is not enough data to tell whether or not their numbers are recovering, and they are listed as 'endangered'.

Bryde's whales are named after John Bryde, a Norwegian consul to South Africa, who, in 1919, helped set up the first whaling post in Durban on South Africa's east coast. Like seis Bryde's are also relatively lean – which is why they prefer these warmer waters – and they too were less profitable than their better insulated counterparts and only became a target for whalers after the more lucrative whales began to diminish. But, eventually, their numbers began to decline too, though today their recovery has been impressive. Their global population is thought to be ninety thousand and a healthy enough number not to be considered endangered.

Although most dolphins are not endangered, there are some that are. Off New Zealand's North Island coast there is just one pod of Maui's dolphins who, like the equally small and also rare Hector's dolphins, are only found in New Zealand waters. The Maui pod is down to a total number of forty-five. With only ten of those mature females they are more at risk of extinction than any other dolphin. And since calves are born only every two to four years (which is the usual span for all cetaceans whatever their size) population growth is a slow process. To make matters worse pervasive chemical pollution, and hormone-disrupting synthetic chemicals in particular, effect fertility. Fishing is another hazard, or more precisely what the fishing industry calls bycatch, which means caught by mistake. And, since Maui's like to keep close to shore, another potentially lethal threat is boat strikes.

But Maui's aren't the only dolphins who are on the most endangered cetaceans list. Hector's dolphins number seven thousand, at most. The Ganges River Dolphin population is about two thousand; the Baiji, or Indus River Dolphins, about one thousand; and Vaquitas, who are taxonomically porpoises and only found in the northern parts of the Gulf California in Mexico, number just five hundred and sixty. Entanglement in fishing gear is largely to blame.

However, thanks to the ban on commercial whaling some whale populations are clearly making a remarkable comeback. But the consequences of the whaling era live on: seven out of the thirteen great whale species are still either 'endangered' or 'vulnerable'.

But now there are other hazards that are more varied and, potentially, just as deadly, as commercial whaling ever was.

4

Nursery grounds

"Suddenly a mighty mass emerged from the water, and shot up perpendicularly into the air. It was the whale."
Miriam Coffin or *The Whale Fisherman,* Joseph C. Hart 1835

Off the west coast of Central America one hundred and fifty blue whales are spread out over the Costa Rica Dome or, to describe it more precisely, the Costa Rica Thermal Convection Dome.

Covering an area of roughly nine hundred miles by three hundred miles the Dome's position varies depending on where the winds, tides and currents are driving warm water down and cold water up – up from the underwater mountains of the Pacific Corridor. The movement of the water carries compounds (that include nitrates, phosphates, silicates and phytoplankton) up to the Ocean's top layer, a richness of nutrients that, at the very bottom of the marine food chain, supports a wealth of life above. Here the waters teem with such an abundance of marine species they make The Dome one of Earth's most 'bio-diverse' habitats and its only unceasing upwelling; a continuous food supply

There are fish in profusion including tuna, sharks and eels; marlin, manta rays and sailfish. Dolphins are also in huge numbers: hundreds of thousands of short-beaked common dolphins, spinner and spotted dolphins and short-finned pilot whales. The Dome's waters also serve as a spawning ground for the giant red squid that sperm whales like to feed on. They are also home to several species of sea turtles including leatherbacks, the largest of all marine reptiles, and the most endangered. And huge numbers of sea birds come to feed here too.

For the eastern North Pacific blue whales - whose total population is around twelve hundred - the never ending source of krill is the main draw and the reason they like to feed, mate and give birth in these warm tropical waters. Some have even made their permanent home here. But they are not the only great whales. Sei, fin, humpback and sperm whales are occasional visitors.

Aerial views of blue whales show how graceful and athletic they look. Their long, tapering, stream-lined shape seems to belie the massiveness of their vital statistics. These are the largest animals that have ever lived: over one hundred feet long when fully grown, the length of a space shuttle. The heaviest animals that have ever existed: one hundred and fifty tons, twice the take-off weight of a Boeing 737 (and far larger than even the biggest and heaviest dinosaurs whose top weight was about thirty-five tons). A tongue weighing six thousand pounds, the weight of a mature African female elephant. A four-chambered heart roughly the weight of a VW Beetle, about one thousand pounds, that contains about seven tons of blood carried by blood vessels large enough for a human to slither through; that beats, on average, six times a minute, with a sound that carries for at least two miles. A lung capacity of, more or less, one thousand gallons. A mouth big enough to hold one hundred people (the only mouths that are larger belong to the Arctic bowhead whales). Whose vocalizations are one hundred and eighty-eight decibels at source, with frequencies down to fourteen Hertz (and well below the range of human hearing whose lowest limit is twelve Hertz), a low-pitched rumbling that can travel from one side of an ocean to the other, and the second loudest animal sound on Earth. (Only the sperm whales' clicks are louder). Of all Earth's animals the fastest-growing. And, with a lifespan of eighty to ninety years, one of the longest lived - the record so far is one hundred and ten years (but beaten by bowheads who can live for over two hundred years).

Three hundred feet below the ocean's surface the marine world is blue-tinged. The light from above shimmers on the whales' silhouettes and gives them a mottled blue-grey-whitish glimmer - the blue of their name. But in this light you cannot see that their undersides are a yellowish green, a colour that comes from a layer of microscopic algae that gives blue whales their other name: sulphur bottoms.

Cruise was born in May. After an eleven month gestation he had, like all sea mammals, arrived tail first with eyes wide open. Within ten seconds his mother, Nessa, had guided him to the surface to take his first breath. He was twenty-five feet long, a quarter of Nessa's length, and his three ton, newborn weight was about the same as a mature rhinoceros. Even on the day of his birth he was larger than almost all of Earth's land animals.

To ease his passage into the world his baleen plates had been soft but in just a few hours they had stiffened and he had become a perfectly formed, smaller version of his adult self. His dorsal fins and flukes had also been flaccid to begin with, and although he swam awkwardly at first he was not so ungainly that he couldn't go the surface to breathe and send up his baby spouts.

Since then Cruise has grown at a phenomenal rate, for no other young animal grows as quickly as a blue whale calf. Putting on fourteen stones a day, eight pounds an hour, each week his weight doubled and he grew one and half feet.

When he was hungry he nudged Nessa' s nipples. She has two and they are an impressive size: seven and a half foot long and over two and half feet in circumference. They are near the rear of her abdomen and, except when she is nursing, concealed in the ninety or so pleats that run from her lower jaw to her belly.

But for Cruise - since whales have no lips - suckling is not an option. Nessa's nursing method is to squirt her milk in short sharp bursts directly into his mouth. It is delivered in prodigious quantities, about fifty gallons a day to begin with.

But this is not milk as we know it. Its consistency is of loose runny cheese, a sort of tooth-paste texture, thick and sticky enough to prevent it dissolving in water. Its nutrient content is also very different from cow's milk that is eighty per cent water, three and a half per cent protein and never more than five per cent fat. Whale's milk is of a whole different order: half fat, eleven per cent protein and more solid than liquid, for whales, despite their watery world, do not drink. A chemical breakdown of blubber delivers their fluids.

Now, at seven months, Cruise is gulping down one hundred and fifty gallons of Nessa's fat-rich, calorie-laden, milk a day. He is largely unaware of its fishy smell (a smell that was so familiar to the old whalers) as the olfactory sense of baleen whales is very weak (and toothed whales have none at all).

When he was smaller he would pester Nessa by climbing onto her flukes and sliding down her back, often stopping on top of her blowhole. Often he got over-excited and the only way she could calm him down was to roll on her back, grab hold of him and clasp him between her flippers until he relaxed.

But now he is less frivolous. In these seven months he has grown twenty five feet which makes him fifty feet long and twenty-three tons, over half his mature, adult size. But he will never reach the proportion of most females as female baleen whales are invariably larger than males.

Soon Cruise will be weaned - though some cows' nurse their calves for a year or more - and he and Nessa will go their separate ways. When he is between five and ten years old he will reach sexual maturity even though he may not be fully grown by then. From the time he leaves Nessa he will spend most of his time alone for, unlike other baleen whales, blue whales seem happy not to search out others, or, if they do, only for short amounts of time. Only mothers and calves are inseparable, and then only until their calf is weaned. But although the whales might be miles apart from each other they are never out of contact. All over the oceans they send out their calls, songs that might come from hundreds of feet deep or carry from one side of a continent to another.

As long as Nessa stays healthy and uninjured she might well live into her nineties. In all that time she will remain fertile. She will calve at two to four year intervals, though the older she becomes the wider the gap as her fertility gradually declines, for menopause (a routine stop to breeding) is rare in the animal world and, as far as is known, occurs only in orcas, short-finned pilot whales, humans, and, perhaps, elephants.

Little is known about the mating habits of blue whales and neither has anyone ever witnessed either their coupling or a blue whale birth. But penis size is not a mystery. With a length of eight to ten feet and a diameter of about one foot this is a dimension that can be added to the blue whales' long list of superlatives: not surprisingly it is, of all animals, the largest. Though not if you are going for penis to body ratio. That would be the barnacle. Since barnacles live their lives firmly attached to whatever they are attached to they need a phallus that is able to reach another, equally immobile, fellow crustacean.

However, a blue whale's penis is good for more than procreation. The old whalers used to make aprons out of the foreskin which, being long enough to reach the ground, gave good protection from the blood and oil when the crew were skinning whales. And because the penis has a bone (as do the penises of most mammals and all primates except humans) the Inuits once used them for sled runners and as clubs for hunting. But it is not just the blue whales' penis size that reaches mega proportions. Testicles weigh between one hundred and one hundred and fifty pounds - each. And at every coupling thirty to forty pints of sperm is ejaculated - about five gallons; enough to wash out the sperm of another whale.

Monogamy is rare in the animal world and great whales seem to be no exception. It is likely that as soon as coitus is finished blue whale bulls, like all whale species, swim away in their graceful and uncommitted fashion while cows stay where they are, and wait for the next male that shows an interest.

Unlike the other great whales blue whales continue to feed during their winter breeding season and for that reason they like to be in places where they can feed all year round. But the others: the finbacks and seis; the right whales, humpbacks and greys, the Brydes and minkes usually choose breeding grounds where food is in scant supply. This means, in spite of all the energy they use travelling to their nursery grounds and the energy needed for lactation, they spend four or five months eating almost nothing at all. Needless to say blubber is lost by the ton.

There are several signs that there are whales at the Dome. The reek of musty, fish-tainted old breath are proof that they are feeding. As are trails of watery orange faeces that look like vast, underwater distress signals. A clue that the whales are blue whales are their forty to fifty foot spumes.

When blue whales are resting they float close to the surface breathing several times an hour. Every five to twenty minutes, through blowholes that resemble a twenty inch human nostril (with an added refinement of a splash guard to keep water out) their breaths erupt with explosive force sending up great jets of vapour that look like monochrome fireworks as the sunlight shimmers through the spray. Then, with stale air expelled and blood re-oxygenated, a whale might make a slight hunch of the back; reveal a glimpse of dorsal fin (which, being just one foot high, is more a swept back bump than a fin); and, with a downward thrust of their flukes, slide beneath the water. The only visible sign that they have been there is their fluke print: a twenty-five foot wide, silky-smooth disc, lying on the surface in unmistakable contrast to the ripples all around. Each whale leaves a distinct pattern, as unique as a human fingerprint.

But the blues can, if they need to, take in enough air to last for well over an hour. That tends to be their usual practice on and off throughout the day when they dive down three hundred and fifty feet to feed. But there are times when they dive deeper still, down to sixteen hundred feet, to where the abyssal zone - the oceans' largest and deepest habitat – begins, and is as deep as some krill go. After a few powerful strokes of their flukes to get them on their way the whale relaxes into an oxygen-saving glide. For a dive this deep, thanks to flexible ribs, their chest compresses; lungs collapse; and air is compacted and forced into the windpipe and out of the bloodstream leaving no dissolved nitrogen in the blood that would turn into bubbles as air decompressed after a deep dive - what humans know as 'the bends' or decompression sickness.

With mouths wide open the whales lunge into huge schools of krill. Thanks to a head one quarter the length of their body, when jaws are open wide and throat pleats fully expanded, a blue whale can swallow a volume of krill and water as large as themselves. In a single gulp a weight of over one hundred and fifty tons. With a mouth so full the change in their shape acts like a drag and, just for a moment, stops them in their tracks. Then pushing their tongue upwards and forcing the water out of their mouths they filter their catch through three hundred and twenty pairs of black baleen plates, each edged with dark grey bristles and over three feet long. In one gulp, one thousand pounds of krill, half a million calories. About four mouthfuls every ten minutes. Every day perhaps six tons, about three to four percent of their body weight.

But at night the krill come up to the surface and then almost no effort is needed to scoop them up. As the whales glide effortlessly through the water the wide arcs of their bow waves shine white in the moonlight.

Krill means small fry in Norwegian and they are just about exclusively what blue whales live on. And both - the baleen whales and the krill - have quite a lot in common. Each is extreme in size: the one massive, the other minute. Both are filter feeders and have combs that act like sieves; the whales' filters are on the edge of their baleen plates and the krills' on their five, front, mini-limbs that look like downward facing antenna. Both are prodigious feeders: the krill feed on plankton (that includes the larvae of marine invertebrates and fish, including the larvae of krill) and the whales feed on krill, which also means that they both feed on short food chains, the efficient sort of food networks where little energy is lost by being transferred along multiple links, such as from plants to herbivores, from herbivores to carnivores, and from smaller carnivores up to the big, apex predators at the top.

Here at the Dome, amongst the blues, there is considerable coming and going. A good layer of blubber - about a quarter of a blue whale's body weight is blubber- means that the whales often get too warm in these tropical waters. It seems their cooling system – that sends blood to flukes and pectoral fins to release heat into the water - is not quite up to scratch. One reason is that blue whales' pectoral fins are relatively small. Being thin and just twelve foot long they are only about fifteen per cent of their body size which makes this method of cooling off less efficient than for those whose pectorals are considerably larger (like humpbacks', for instance, whose pectoral fins are one third of their body length). Heading for the mid latitude cooler water can be a refreshing relief.

Travelling at a steady fourteen miles an hour, with graceful strokes of their immense, muscular flukes they power through the water as gracefully as birds on the wing. This is the only time – when they are moving rapidly between feeding grounds – that they do not feed. Only the nursing mothers tend not to leave. With calves taking in milk at a ravenous rate they need to keep their energy up.

Soon Cruise will be setting out on his own, but he will always be tuned into the calls of other whales. Thanks to his size he has a good chance of survival - though the longer calves stay with their mothers the more they learn about coping with the oceans' hazards -and the better their chances. His only natural predators are killer whales who, despite their guile, he has a good chance of outrunning, or at least repelling, since just one flick of his flukes could be lethal.

Far more threatening are man-made hazards. He will always be at risk of collision with boats and ships. Or ingesting plastic debris. Or entanglement in fishing equipment. Or poisoning from pollution. Or disorientation from noise. All consequences of human's industrial lifestyle.

5

Life's a Circus

"Animals can communicate quite well. And they do.
And generally speaking they are ignored."
Alice Walker *The Color Purple*

In the Sea of Okhotsk all twenty members of the killer whale pod are lined up, flipper to flipper, all facing the same way and parallel to each other. This is the killer-whale, the orca-way, of enjoying a welcome pause after a long hunt. But they cannot afford to be layabouts: their healthy appetites require five hundred pounds of food a day and so they never rest for long. Most or their days and nights are spent hunting. Sometimes the pod travels over a hundred miles on hunts that can last for up to fourteen hours.

Today Kaito is on breathing duty. The others are deeply half asleep, half in the sense that only one side of a cetacean's brain ever sleeps at any one time. Two sides at once would be to forget to breathe since cetaceans, like humans, cannot breathe under water. But, unlike humans, their breathing is a conscious action, a vital undertaking, always on their minds. Choices have to be made: whether to breathe once a minute or not for twenty minutes, depending.

So when Kaito goes up to the surface to breathe they all follow suit. Every four minutes they rise together and their dorsal fins break out of the water in unison, fins that are as unique and individual as their owners' characters. The largest, straighter, fins belong to the bulls and they rise six feet above the surface. The backward-curving fins, that are half that size of the males, belong to the cows. The cows' body sizes are also smaller, around four tons and rarely more than twenty feet, while some bulls can weigh over six tons and grow to thirty feet.

The orcas' rhythmic breathing sends up spumes at twenty second intervals and so, at the surface of this part of the Sea of Okhotsk, fountains of vapour - bushy-shaped, steaming mixtures of water and mucus - spout up into the atmosphere. Twenty orcas breathing peacefully, lulled, under Kaito's leadership, into a calm and tranquil symmetry.

But the pod's relaxed demeanour belies their killer instinct. For orcas are one of the world's most powerful predators and one of the largest warm blooded carnivores on Earth. Not for nothing are they called killer whales (though they are not really whales but the largest member of the dolphin family). Orcas are also fast. Their top speed of thirty miles an hour - even if only for short bursts - makes them among the fastest of all marine animals. Not for nothing have they been called the cheetahs of the sea. But their cruising speed - eight miles an hour - is more leisurely.

To be known as whales or cheetahs might not be strictly correct but the killer reference unquestionably applies. These largest of all dolphins are awesome strategists and cooperation is the name of the game. With ruthless efficiency, in deadly pods, they pool resources and work together. Up to forty might hunt side by side as other orcas from different groups join forces.

Like wolf packs on land they stalk their prey. Depending on its size they might swallow their catch whole, or, with their four inch teeth, tear off chunks regardless of whether their quarry is dead or alive: seals, sea lions, squid, octopus, sea birds, leatherback turtles and even sharks; though when it comes to the great white they tend to take the precaution of paralysing the ferocious fish first by flipping them upside down before tearing into their flesh. They will even target a polar bear if the opportunity arises as well as other dolphins and whales, with minkes a particular favourite.

The adults' co-operation is honed by experience which means they have no need to send instructions to each other as they home in on their prey, Up until then all is stealth and quiet. As the orcas' attacks take place, the young orcas stay on the side lines, watching and learning. But once the adults have got hold of their victim the chattering begins: clicking and whistling, squeaks, squawks and shrills: as sociable a sound as any heard at a human dinner party. Their strong regional dialects, their own distinctive way of expressing themselves, is another similarity to humans and all other cetaceans.

The pod's choice of quarry depends on availability, personal choice and the oceans they are in. The orcas of the Pacific Northwest mostly live on salmon which they swallow whole, in a single gulp. Pods in other oceans have considered the tongues of grey whales a delicacy, tongues that can weigh up to several tons and are dense with muscle and protein. Even blue whales are a common target and one quarter of the world's blues have the scars to prove it - and stories to tell as a result. Like the sixty foot blue whale who was attacked by a thirty-strong orca pod. Some attacked from the front, some from the rear; there were orcas leaping on his back and others at his sides, all taking bites of his flesh and blubber. The attack lasted five hours.

But when it comes to humans only rarely have any been attacked by orcas in the wild (though in captivity it's a different story). No-one knows why wild orcas rarely target humans. A diver who was pulled into the ocean by a wild orca was not, it seemed, to the animal's taste. She was spat out and survived. And, once, so another story goes, an orca pod protected humans from sharks and saved their lives, as if, it was surmised, some sort of empathy exists.

And so orcas have two sides to their characters. On the one they are deadly killers. On the other they are gentle, calm and sociable. To them home is where the pod is. Family life is all important, the company of their family group - grandparents, sons and daughters, all the generations and both sexes, always together. Few other animals stay with their mothers for their entire lives as orcas do with theirs.

Being apex predators - that is, predators that have no predators – killer whales feel confident of their position and certain they are at the top of their game. But they are wrong.

They can never know until it is too late just how endangered the lives of some of them have become. Or how great a price is on their heads.

The history of their value to humans goes back many decades, to the time when it was discovered that cetaceans could be kept in circuses, circuses where the star attractions would become killer whales.

The first orca ever to be caught alive was a sick and confused female that was found in Newport Harbour, off California in 1961. Her captors took her to Marineland in California, a large-scale aquarium, a so-called ocanarium. But after two days in a concrete tank she smashed her head into the tank wall and died.

The second orca wasn't meant to be taken alive. In 1964 word had gone out that a dead killer whale was wanted as a model for an artist who had been commissioned to make a full size sculpture for a marine museum. It didn't take long before a suitable orca was sighted - and the chase was on. The orca was harpooned, but when that didn't kill her, she was shot. But she survived the gun shots too. Then, still alive, she was towed - dragged by the harpoon line that had caught in the base of her dorsal fin - for twenty miles, for sixteen hours, in choppy seas. She was called Moby Doll and displayed at Burrard Drydocks in Vancouver in Canada. But after eighty-seven days she died. Only then was it realised that she was a he.

Next, in June 1965, a young twenty two foot male orca was found entangled in a salmon fishing net off Namu, in Canada's British Colombia. The fishermen knew that there was now a price for blackfish, which was what they called orcas. So they decided to tow him in alive. They were paid US$8,000, just enough to cover the cost of their damaged nets.

The orca was put in a floating pen and towed to Seattle, a journey of four hundred and fifty miles. On the fourth day of the journey there was a sound of screaming: thirty or forty orcas had come to his rescue. They kept charging at the sea cage, stopping just a fraction before hitting it. But what could they do? Eventually they abandoned hope - all except a female and two calves who stayed with him for one hundred and fifty miles. Because they found it so hard to leave him it's thought they must have been his mother and siblings.

He was put in a sea pen in the Seattle Public Aquarium and called Namu after the place he was caught. It was said that the public fell in 'love' with Namu and he became a huge attraction. In the first two months one hundred and twenty thousand visitors came to see him. One day the Aquarium's owner decided - against all advice - to get in the tank with him. The Aquarium owner was amazed to find out how kind and gentle he was - not the killer everyone expected. After that they did shows together and Namu became the first orca ever to perform in captivity. But he was often heard screeching loudly and whales that were passing by his pen at Sea Cove would return his calls. After eleven months Namu became ill. A few days later he hurled himself as fast as he could at into the side of his pen, and died.

Having found there was a great deal of money to be made from captive killer whales, the quest for more began. Top of the wanted list were calves, preferably weaned and between two and five years old, as young animals are easier to transport and handle. And also – because it was thought, and still is - that young animals are better at adapting to captivity.

But there is only one way to capture young calves and that is to round up entire pods. It's a huge undertaking and aeroplanes and helicopters are usually set out to spot them. The moment the hunters are tipped off they take up the chase in speed boats. When the boats begin to close in the crew let off explosives to panic the pod and make it easier to drive the terrified animals into huge nets; some cover three acres. For the final capture, the ropes come out. And then the havoc really begins. Orcas scream. Humans yell. Mother orcas become trapped in the nets trying to save their babies who often drown. Orca families are rent apart as the targeted animals are taken and hoisted up into the boats.

Between 1965 and 1977 there were nineteen known orca hunts. Two hundred and sixty two orcas were caught and fifty young taken. In their first year of captivity sixteen of those fifty died.

Namu wasn't the only orca celebrity. In October 1965, the same year as Namu's capture, Shamu was caught when her mother was harpooned from a helicopter. He was the first orca ever to be intentionally caught and it was intended that Namu and Shamu would be company for each other. But they didn't get on and Shamu was sold to SeaWorld in San Diego.

In those days, in the late 1960s, Shamu became the longest living captive orca; she survived for over thirteen months. She was also the first to attack a trainer. For some reason she singled out those in bikinis, never any wearing wetsuits. After she had turned on several scantily-clad trainers she was retired. She died four months later, in August 1971. She was nine years old.

But the public weren't told of her death and the Shamu shows went on. The name was the same but the animals were different - a common mass impersonation in marine animal parks. It's an easy stunt to pull because humans can't recognize how individual cetaceans are. In one park a famous pilot whale was in fact thirteen different animals – clear proof, as if one was needed, that for orcas, and all other captive marine animals, being kept in a dolphinarium is as good as a death sentence: a death that is long drawn-out as animals die from grief, stress and abject frustration.

Amongst all these stories of lives cut short there is one exception: Lolita, the longest living imprisoned orca. She was captured in 1970 when she was four. She belonged to Puget Sound's L-Pod and when the eighty-strong pod was rounded up in Penn Cove in August 1970 she was one of seven calves taken. Ever since she has lived in the Miami Seaquarium in a concrete tank. Two of the other calves captured at the same time were sent to marine parks in Japan; another was sent to Texas; another to the UK; one to France; and one to Australia. In five years they had all died.

For ten years Lolita was penned with Hugo who had already been at Seaquarium for two years. They belonged to the same clan and like Lolita Hugo had been with his mother when he was captured. He was three years years old. For ten years the two twenty foot orcas lived together in a tank sixty feet wide, eighty feet long and twenty feet deep. Hugo's top dorsal fin had curled over - a sign of depression and ill health in orcas. On March 4,1980, after twelve years performing three times a day, Hugo killed himself by repeatedly smashing his head against the tank wall.

Ever since Lolita has been alone in their tank. After Hurricane Irma hit Florida in 2017 a video taken from a drone showed she was still alive in the pool just four times her length, in water that one witness described as 'like a cesspool' (probably because the filtering system had gone down in the storm). She has been in captivity for over forty-five years.

Shamu was not the only captive orca that lived that up to the name 'killer'. In November 1983 an orca, who was later called Tilikum, was captured near Iceland and taken to Sealand of the Pacific, a run-down marine park in British Colombia. He was put in a tank with two female orcas, Haida and Nootka. The tank was fifty feet wide, one hundred feet long and thirty-five feet deep. Tilikum was forced to perform eight times a day, seven days a week. As if that wasn't hard enough Haida and Nootka bullied him; yet every night, for fourteen hours, all three orcas were kept together, in a small metal-sided cage. So perhaps it was no surprise that Tilikum suffered from exhaustion and stomach ulcers. And then, in what must have been desperate frustration, he finally lived up to his name and killed.

In 1991 Katie Byrne, a trainer, fell into the pool that held all three orcas. Tilikum got hold of her, tossed her to Haida and Nootka, and the three orcas continued tossing her to each other until she drowned.

When Sealand closed in 1992 Tilikum was to moved to Florida, to SeaWorld in Orlando. In 1999 he killed again. Daniel Dukes, a spectator, had managed to stay in the marine park after it had closed. The next day he was found drowned, with cuts all over him and stripped of his clothes.

A year later Tilikum killed a third time, another trainer called Dawn Brancheau. He grabbed her ponytail, pulled her into the pool, broke her bones, scalped her, dismembered her and, finally, drowned her. After that he was kept in isolation for thirteen months, presumably a broken and demented orca, like so many others. The great number of distraught animals is made clear in the records kept at marine mammal parks. Hundreds of entries describe orcas biting, ramming, lunging, pulling, pinning and threatening. Their message couldn't be clearer.

As the United States haven't issued a permit to capture wild orcas since 1989 the demand for new orcas has been met by breeding programmes. In the same way that the reproductive cycles of farm animals are managed so they breed continuously, the breeding cycles of female orcas are manipulated with drugs and they are impregnated by artificial insemination. WhenTilikium was moved to Florida in 1992 another role was added to his curriculum. He was used as a stud killer whale: a sperm donor. Orca stud bulls are trained to lie on their backs and present their penis, and then, like stud bulls for the dairy and meat industries, masturbated to extract their semen. Over half of the calves born to female orcas at SeaWorld had been artificially impregnated with his sperm.

Tilikum died in 2017 after being ill for some time. He was probably thirty-six. He had been the largest killer whale ever to have been in captivity: twenty-two feet and well over six tons; when he was captured he had been thirteen feet and about two years old. For over thirty years he had preformed without a break, except for thirteen months after he killed Dawn Brancheau.

The US might no longer sanction capturing wild orcas but there are many countries that do. With marine parks in sixty-three countries there is no shortage of demand for performing animals Orcas, pilot whales, beluga whales, bottle-nose dolphins, seals and seal lions; they are all on the wanted list.

Marine parks go by several names: dolphinariums, marine animal parks, oceanariums, animal theme parks, aquariums. But whatever they are called the conditions are all the same. In bare concrete pools these wild marine animals are condemned to lives as different from their ocean world as is possible to imagine. Not only have they endured the shock and trauma of capture; been wrenched from their mothers and family groups;

and suffered the ordeal of transportation. Now they are doomed to spend the rest of their lives cramped for space, in chlorinated water, often with no escape from sweltering sun, where their bio-sonar must bounce off the sides in a deafening and maddening way. What these places really are is circuses in which the acrobats are wild sea mammals. Japan has the most: fifty-seven; China has forty-four; in Russia there are thirty-four; and Mexico has twenty-four. And all a pitiful contrast to the freedom of the oceans where their wild counterparts travel long distances and dive down hundreds of feet to catch their prey, all in the familiar company of their family pods.

The signs of stress are clear. The imprisoned orcas chew at the metal gates and the sides of their concrete pools until their teeth are worn down, or broken. The so-called 'remedy' for broken teeth is to extract them with power drills. Their suffering makes them ill. It weakens immune systems and they become susceptible to a raft of diseases such as haemorrhagic pneumonia; intestinal gangrene; pulmonary abscesses; stomach ulcers; kidney disease; cardiovascular failure; septicaemia; influenza. The list is long. The most visible sign of their ill health and stress is dorsal collapse, when their dorsal fin flops to one side.

But the signs of strain invite no pity from the park owners. They have just one interest: keeping the animals alive. And so medication is routinely dispensed. The doses are stuffed into chunks of gelatine that include antibiotics to help cure and stave off disease; valium-type drugs to help calm them; and pain killers to ease the pain of damaged teeth.

The average life span of wild orcas is sixty to seventy years. In marine animal parks seven years is standard, and would be shorter still if they weren't kept alive with regular doses of a raft of medicinal drugs.

But what really keeps the shows going is the paying public. As long as people buy tickets the performances continue - and the animals suffer the consequences. In the UK, when people realised the cruelty involved, they stopped going and the last show closed in 1993. Now keeping sea mammals for entertainment is banned, as it is in many other countries;

Bolivia, Chile, Costa Rica, Croatia, Cyprus, Greece, Hungary, Slovenia, India and Nicaragua are just some of them.

Where shows do continue it seems audiences are easily duped. Some believe they are learning about the animals they watch performing . But do these spectators really think that in the wild animals wave to humans; or go up to them and shake their hands; or splash them with water; and willingly allow trainers to balance on what are often called noses but are, zoolologically 'rostrums' - as in a beak, or beak like part. Some spectators believe the animals perform because they think it's fun. Others think that the smiley faces of bottlenose dolphins prove that the animals enjoy what they do, though, since dolphins can't move their facial muscles, they couldn't smile even if they wanted do. The 'smile' is simply the line of their jaws - jaws that are lined with sharp teeth for tearing fish and squid, and are lethally efficient.

All cetaceans have an aggressive side and also a good sense of fun – but in their natural habitat; not in marine parks. Orcas are no exception. In the wild they are extremely curious - reckless even - since not being used to predators caution is not something they tend to practice. But games are. It takes very little to encourage them to join in, like the time humans threw snowballs at an orca pod. In no time the animals were throwing back chunks of ice. Or the time a group of orcas teased humans by edging away objects that humans were trying get hold of by pushing them barely out of reach. Over and over again. But performing in captivity is not for fun. The reality is that the animals perform because if they don't they don't get fed.

The idea that dophinariums are havens could hardly be further from the truth. The ocean explorer, Jean-Michal Cousteau, has likened keeping orcas in dolphinariums to keeping a human prisoner blindfolded in a jail cell. All energy and exuberance stifled as the animals suffer appalling misery.

But the lure of money overcomes any mercy and the shows go on. Captured orcas can fetch millions of dollars and ticket sales millions more. Once, in the 1970s, it was thought that the days of wild capture were over but now its seems hunting has resumed. Demand is high, not least because the number of oceanariums in Russia and China is growing. China wants more marine animals and the Russians are supplying them. Between 2008 and 2010, in the Sea of Okhotsk, the Russians caught sixty beluga whales which they exported to China. In 2013, also in the Sea of Okhotsk , where the orca population is an estimated three thousand, seven orcas were caught on two separate hunts. But the exact figures aren't known. This is a business shrouded in secrecy.

For all the orcas' intelligence - whose brains are bigger than any other dolphin, and the second heaviest brain on Earth, second only to sperm whales' - they have little hope against human technology. The chance of avoiding spotter planes or outpacing speed boats is unlikely, and their curiosity doesn't help either. The sight of killer whales bow-riding the stern waves of boats shows how much they like to have fun. But how are they to know which boats come intent on capture. How can they tell that the dumped fresh herrings are bait to entice their pods into nets. And that the hunters are well aware that where one orca goes the others follow, and that if any fellow pod member is in danger the others are sure to come, as they always do, to the rescue.

Then the mayhem begins – and all because customers pay to be entertained by marine mammals in circuses.

6

Whales Have Ears

"A deaf whale is a dead whale."

Tim Donaghy,
senior research specialist with Greenpeace

In Moby Dick Herman Melville marvels at the size – or rather, the lack of size - of a whale's ear, which is just behind the eye. He was just as surprised to find that whales' ears have no ear lobe. He described a sperm whales ear as an opening so small that "into the hole itself you can hardly insert a quill". And noted that the right whale's ear is covered by a membrane and not visible at all. But Melville was in no doubt that all whales have acute hearing even if their ears are "smaller than a hare's".

Like humans all cetaceans have semicircular, fluid-filled canals in their inner ear, that help keep them balanced. But the ear canals of cetaceans – even a blue whales' - are remarkably small, about three times smaller than those of humans' or any other land animal. So what are they for? The theory is that they stop cetaceans becoming dizzy when they do their acrobatic jumps.

Ear wax on the other hand is very different. The ear canals of all cetaceans are plugged with dense wax though, as there is no connection between their ear canals and ear drums, being blocked with wax has no affect on their hearing. But this doesn't mean they can't hear. In fact cetaceans have extremely sensitive hearing but theirs are aquatic ears, ears that have evolved to listen to sounds under water, not in air. In air sounds are transmitted to the brains of land mammals and birds through tiny bones in the middle ear. For marine mammals sounds are processed very differently.

In toothed cetaceans it seems sound waves are channelled along the lower jaw to the inner ear, while in baleen whales it appears they pass through the skull bone rather than the jaw bone, and also through the head's soft tissue. In a way the whole of a cetaceans' head is an ear, an ear in which there are several auditory pathways rather than a single canal as land animals have. And fish too also send and receive sounds through an assortment of sound-conducting parts like bones, whiskers and swim bladders.

No-one is absolutely sure exactly how whales' hearing works but what is certain is that it is extremely acute and has a great range: twelve octaves compared to a human's eight. But in the whale's ocean world the kind of air-filled ear that land animals have would be useless, just as whales' ears probably can't pick up sounds when their heads are above the water. Not only are aquatic ears unlike land ears, but the way sounds travel in water is also completely different. Since water is five times denser than air sounds carry faster, further and – in what would be confusing for humans if they were able to hear under water - in all directions.

To humans the ocean world appears to be a quiet place, but that's only because most underwater sounds are out of our hearing range. But if you had the ears to hear you would find there are more natural sounds in the marine world than on the land above and that the oceans are full of natural sounds. Fish grunt, grind, sing and scrape. Cod fish croak; gurnards croon; conger eels belch, moan and groan. Crustaceans (crabs, shrimps and lobsters) click, crackle and snap. Fish shoals swish. Bubbles pop. Barnacles click as they open and close. There are thuds, hummings, rustlings and tickings as animals move, hunt, mate and fight. There are the rattlings of pebbles and the hissing of sand as the tides and currents stir up the sea floor, dragging them first one way and then another. There is the swooshing of water through fronds of kelp. There are reverberations from wind, rain and storms (even down in the deepest depth the low muffled roar of hurricanes can be heard). There are booms from earthquakes. volcanoes and calving glaciers. There are the clicks of cetaceans sending out their bio-sonar. And there are the songs of whales that spread far out over the oceans.

But some parts of the oceans are becoming quieter. On some coral reefs - as the climate changes and acid levels rise, or as trawlers scrape reefs clean – animals are dying and the sounds of some of what were once the noisiest places in the oceans are being wiped out. And where bottom trawlers have ravaged great tracts of seabed they have left in their wake vast areas of wasteland with all life gone.

To hear this other-worldly soundscape humans need technical assistance as many marine sounds are beyond our hearing range. Without amplifying devices we wouldn't know about the low frequency pulses, the groans, moans, sighs, roars and deep thumping throbs of the great baleen whalebone whales, though their short-range communications are within our grasp. Hydrophones are particularly helpful but even then many sounds are only audible after calculations have been made, frequencies altered and timings changed. For instance a blue whale's song, the loudest animal sound in the world, has to be speeded up by a factor of five before humans can hear it.

But we are able to hear most of the toothed cetaceans' wide range of high pitched clicks and whistles that sound like morse code, although their lowest and highest sounds are beyond humans' natural hearing. But even though we can hear the sound of their sonar pulses - the pulses that show the animals what their eyes cannot - we don't have the capacity to understand them. But for the animals, when their pings echo back and vibrate along their jaws to the ear canal, their brain analyses the vibrations and gives them a three dimensional view - a view that is detailed to the nth degree: the shape of bays, coves and inlets; the distance to the seabed and the layout of the seafloor; all the objects both on and beneath it; the texture of those objects, whether they are hard or soft; animate or inanimate. Their super-human, echo-sounding sonar even shows them other animals' internal parts, details like skeletons, lungs and hearts. And whether what they are seeing is friend, foe or food.

All this information is calculated at a phenomenal rate. It has been estimated that toothed whales can take in and process ten times more data at any one time than humans ever do. Their precision seems just as extraordinary: pour just a teaspoon of water into a captive dolphin's tank and in a fraction of a second the dolphin will mark it exactly.

It was their superfast processing and sonar abilities that gave the United States' Navy the idea of training bottlenose dolphins as minesweepers for their Navy Marine Mammal Program. The dolphins - who are trained in a similar way to dogs by being given rewards for completed tasks - can detect in minutes what humans might take days to find. Another dolphin quality is reliability and trust. But details of their naval experience are scarce. Californian sea lions have also been commandeered for their flawless eyesight that makes them ideal spotters of enemy swimmers. All skills that humans could never match.

The low-pitched songs that the great baleen whales send out, even during deep dives, are the loudest animal sounds in the world but nobody knows whether or not they are part of the echolocation system that their toothed counterparts rely on. Some marine biologists think they are. Others think they aren't. The reasoning of the first rests on the fact that baleen whales, being consumer of small shoaling fish and plankton, don't need a sophisticated hunting aid like their echolocating fellows; and secondly, their jaws lack the sound-carrying fat that the jaws of toothed whales have . But there is a consensus that bowheads - the Greenland or Arctic whales - almost certainly use echolocation to navigate their way under the thick polar ice.

So how do the great baleen whales interpret what is going on around them? Are they guided by water temperature; or by the currents and tides; or, perhaps, by magnet fields. Or do they rely on memory to find their way in their underwater world, a world of diminishing light where luminescence decreases as the depth increases, until, at six hundred and sixty feet the oceans' top, sunlit layer ends, the zone where most of the marine life we have so far identified lives, and the twilight zone begins?

This 'middle pelagic' zone is a dark blue and black place with scarcely any light at all. It's home to a medley of uncanny life, for the animals who live there have had to adapt to tremendous pressure, low temperatures (about 4 °C) and murky darkness. Most are small, dark and thin and many have eyes, teeth and jaws that seem abnormally large. Though they all – like the crabs, snails, eels, worms, starfish fish, squid and octopus - bear a resemblance, albeit a ghoulish one, to their counterparts in the illuminated world above. Some even give off an eerie green light, a glow-in-the-dark bioluminescence that is a product of chemical reaction. But without sunlight for photosynthesis this is a place devoid of plants and so the animals have to get their energy from other sources. Some move into the sunlight zone above to feed. Others eat plant matter that has drifted down from above. And some eat each other. As for the whales who dive this deep; eyesight is of no use in this unlit middle zone, which is why they need biosonar to map their world by sound.

Below the twilight zone, deeper than six and half thousand feet, the midnight or abyssal zone begins (abyssus means "bottomless pit" in Late Latin). Here it is pitch black, the temperature 2 to 3 °C, and the pressure between two hundred and six hundred atmospheres. Like those in the middle pelagic zone the animals that live here have to survive either on the detritus that drifts down from above, or on other animals. Ninety per cent of the ocean is in this, the midnight, zone and it's home to a host of bizarre creatures that never see the light of day. The animals here are grotesque, the stuff of nightmares: the fish and sharks; the crabs and lobsters; the tube worms, starfish and jellyfish; the snails and slugs. And, of course, the giant squid, the deep-dwelling prey of sperm whales. Even these oceans' deepest reaches teem with life. But only sperm whales and Cuvier's beaked whale venture this deep, diving down into the pitch blackness; and then only long enough to catch their prey.

Although all cetaceans have exceptional hearing and most rely on their biosonar to guide them in dim or no light they also have good eyesight. Melville also noted that whales' eyes, like their ears, seem small for such an enormous animal. He likened them to the eyes of a young colt, though in reality they are about the size of a grapefruit, which, in view of the scale of a whale, is indeed, relatively, small.

It seemed to Melville that since a whale's eyes are on the side of a such a vast head they must have only thirty degree vision and be unable to look either directly forwards or directly backwards. And that each eye, being positioned on the side of such an enormous head, must get a completely different view from the other. In other words whales eyes see two different things at once; and nothing at all in front.

Just as water carries noises in a different way from air so light functions differently too: it bends, and in bending falls on an object at an angle. For a human bent light makes depth hard to judge and things in the distance seem blurred so that we aren't able to make out an object's exact position. But cetaceans' eyes have adapted to cope with the refracted light just as they have adapted to cope with the oceans' dim surroundings. Their very large pupils let in even the weakest light which means they can see things that human eyes could never see. And, by narrowing their pupils down to a slit, these eyes can also adapt to bright sunlight so that whales can see just as well at the surface as they can in the oceans' less sunlit zones.

But it's not just ears, eyes and sonar expertise that guide whales. Their skin is also extremely sensitive and serves as yet another navigation aid. Through it they sense the water's turbulence so that they can, for maximum efficiency, adjust their swimming accordingly. This responsive skin began its development fifty million years ago when whales began to evolve from the even-toed ungulates, the Artiodactyla of the early Eocene, named for eos, Greek for dawn. This was the dawn of hoofed animals like pigs, camels and cattle, and also hippopotomuses that share their beginnings with whales. At that time Earth was between 9 and 14°C warmer than it is today and carbon dioxide (CO_2) between one thousand and two thousand parts per million; (today's CO_2 is about four hundred ppm, and rising).

It took these animals a further eight million years to head for the sea and the vestiges of their evolutionary beginnings still remain. Like the land animals they evolved from they breathe air; are warm-blooded; have four chambered hearts; and give birth to live young that feed from mammary glands. They also have remnants of leg and feet bones near the end of their back bone; and remnants of front legs, that look like forearms, wrist bones and fingers, in their flippers. From their hippopotamus-like ancestors they retain a three-chambered stomach (though sperm whales have four) but unlike their land-based mammalian ancestors their skin has become aquadynamic, smooth to prevent drag, but also easily scarred and prone to sunburn. They also have vestiges of the hair that once completely covered them. Some whales have a few isolated hairs around their mouth and blowhole, but the hair on humpbacks, right whales and bowheads is in the form of whiskers and much more noticeable. And all cetacean fetuses have hair on their heads though, by the time they are born, they have lost it.

On humpbacks the traces of their hirsute evolutionary past have developed into oversized hair follicles, golf ball size lumps, called tubercles, out of which grows a single grey hair. To recognise an individual humpback you only have to look at its tubercles. There will be between thirty and sixty and, even though they are always in symmetrical rows, their groupings will be distinct. It's not clear what their tubercles' hairs are for, though suggestions have been made. Perhaps, like cats' whiskers, they are sensory systems and receivers of messages. Maybe they pick up subtle vibrations. And if they do what sort of vibrations? Might they be the throbbing of low-frequency sounds? Or the slight disturbances in the water that are made by prey? Could they pick up electromagnetic fields? Or what? Nevertheless, however good their eyesight; and however useful their skin, whiskers and tubercles; and however explicit their body language, all the jumping and tail slapping, nudging and touching, when it comes to processing information, the primary sense for whales - the sense that is the most important of all their faculties - is hearing. Their world is shaped by sound. Without ears to hear they would be, in effect, deaf and blind: unable to navigate; incapable of tracking food; unable to tell where their calves and each other were; and devoid of understanding what was going on around them.

But whales' ears are more than vital organs, organs without which they could not function. They have stories to tell. Up until now it was whale blubber that scientists examined to find out details of a whale's life, such as their age and what chemicals they might have absorbed. But now the same information has been deduced from earwax - plus a bonus. It holds a record of not just what has been absorbed; but when.

These dense, fat-rich, plugs that build up in whales' ear canals look like striped branches of wood, up to ten inches long and an inch or two in diameter. Like the rings of a tree they are laid down in bands, though in the case of earwax longitudinal bands, with each band representing about six months of time.

Though not all whale species have earplugs, and those that do have varied amounts, there is much to learn from those who do. They tell a whale's age. Stress hormones mark the whale's first mating, the time they reached sexual maturity. Hormone traces disclose a cow's number of pregnancies. The plankton that the whale fed on leaves nitrogen isotopes that tell which seas the whale inhabited and isotopes of carbon and nitrogen divulge the level of those elements in the seawater. Earwax plugs also reveal any toxins the whale might have absorbed.

What has become clear so far is that it is the youngest whales ingest the most toxins, passed on to calves in their mother's milk, milk that might contain residues from those persistent organic pollutants, the so-called POPs that include pesticides (even long-banned DDT) and flame retardants, as well as several other chemicals, and also mercury.

For hundreds of years museums all over the world have collected whales' earwax. The USA's Smithsonian's National Museum of Natural History has one thousand plugs taken from whaling stations during the1950s and 1960's. A comparison with those and the earplugs of more recently deceased whales should be revealing, though nowadays most whale carcases end up on the ocean floor. But their earwax plugs, being partly made of keratin, are denser than bones and last long after a skeleton has decomposed. And so plugs of whales' earwax are another diminutive fraction of the secrets embedded in the ocean floor, in the sediments there that have been forming for aeons.

For nearly four billion years, since the primeval ocean formed, and the Earth had cooled enough for its gases to turn to water and the first rains began to fall, that sediment has been building up. Ever since, all kinds of material - gravel, pebbles, rocks, sand, soil and minerals, including salt - have been migrating seaward, washed down from the land by rivers and rain. Volcanoes have spewed ash into the atmosphere and the rains have washed it down onto the land and into the oceans. The winds have picked up desert sand and exposed top soil, and they too have been picked up by winds and dropped on the land and the seas. Even meteorites that have crash-landed out of space have scattered their galactic debris including metals like iron and nickel, and also iridium which is far more abundant in meteors than on Earth.

The accumulation of these deposits on the ocean floor, thin layer upon thin layer over aeons of geological time, is a process that will continue as long as Earth has seas; and all a treasure trove of Earth's history. Over millions of years, the oldest have become solidified and transformed into sedimentary rocks like sandstones, siltstones and mudrocks, the kind of rocks where fossils are found. But the most profuse contributors to the ocean sediments are the shells and skeletons of marine animals that have been accumulating since they first appeared half a billion years ago. These are limestone's beginnings: those shell-forming organisms like corals, molluscs, brachiopods and snails, remains that have been joined by other prehistoric skeletons, including those of the early whales like Dorudon (meaning spear-toothed) and Basilosaurus (whose body was long and eel-like) who evolved over forty millions years ago, when the ear wax of whales was also at the genesis of its evolution.

But not all these sedimentary rocks are still on the ocean bed. Earth's movements - its continental collisions and the slipping and sliding of tectonic plates - have pushed some ocean floors above the oceans' surface. Even high in the Himalayas marine fossils have been found, including the jawbone of Earth's oldest whale who probably hunted in water but rested and bred on land. The fossil of Himalayacetus subathuensis was thought to be fifty three and half millions old, even older than the whales of the Eocene, like Dorudon and Basilosaurus whose legs began to be superseded by flippers between forty-one and fifty million years ago.

As far as our knowledge of whales is concerned there is still much to be discovered. But one mystery has been solved - a finding that has also benefited the aerodynamic industry.

Dr Frank Fish studies the way marine animals move. In the early 2000s he was in a gift shop looking at a whale sculpture. It seemed to him that it had been incorrectly modelled because the tubercles were on the leading edge of the fins, a concept that went against the aerodynamic assumptions of that time. Just to be sure Dr. Fish double checked. He noticed that if he placed bumps on the leading edge of a blade in a similar pattern to a humpback's tubercles, the bumps channelled the water into streams that flowed off more quickly than off a surface that had no restrictions at all. The result was less drag and more uplift – which helps explains the athleticism of an animal as large and heavy as a humpbacks who weighs as much as six adult elephants.

Inspired by the humpback fins' design Dr. Fish found that when air was similarly channelled on the front edge of a turbine blade it passed over, as water did, more quickly than over a smooth surface. And so wind turbines are now built according to the 'tubercle principle'. Not only do they produce more power at low speed but they are also quieter. And wings of aircraft that are designed in the same way have more lift.

In this instance a whale has benefited industry. But in general mankind's technology has done little to improve the lot of whales.

Ever since fossil fuels took the place of whale oil, drilling for oil has become an industrial priority and the oceans the new frontier. Offshore drilling is happening all over the world: in the Gulf of Mexico; off the coast of California; in the Caspian Sea; the North Sea; off Brazil; off Canada's coasts of Newfoundland and Nova Scotia.; off Russia and the Persian Gulf; off India's coasts, both west and east. And most recently Ghana, the Republic of Côte d'Ivoire, Guinea and Senegal are all new centres of West Africa's oil exploration, the so-called the West African Transform Margin. The large petroleum companies are also looking towards the Arctic. The Russians have already begun extracting oil from the Pechora Sea (in northwest Russia in the south eastern area of the Barents Sea) and plan to increase production there. Coastal and offshore hydraulic fracturing - known as fracking - is also making its effect felt as large amounts of waste, contaminated with toxic chemicals, are spewed out of old oil wells, often accompanied by incessant drilling.

Of all man-made impacts on the oceans it seems that the noise of drilling effects cetaceans most. Pile-driving with huge hammers and unexpected explosions are particularly disturbing and in the worst cases can cause permanent ear damage. But any noise is disrupting. When animals are feeding within hearing range – which, given the distances that sounds carry in water, is more than likely - they are forced away from where they like to be.

The worst noise is made by seismic airguns towed behind ships searching for oil and gas below the ocean floor. The compressed air that the guns blast out is one hundred thousand times more intense than any air that comes out of a jet engine, and at source measures two hundred and fifty decibels. Towed behind ships over huge areas the guns sound off every ten seconds for hours on end. And sometimes the blasts continue for days, and even weeks.

It's said that the explosive sounds injure not just sea mammals but all sorts of other sea life and kill sea turtles and fish, fish eggs and larvae, and force those who can, to leave the area. And because sounds carry over four times faster and more than ten times further in water than in air these noises can carry thousands of miles, across entire ocean basins. Although sounds fade the further they travel and the frequency lessens, the lower the pitch the more similar they become to the songs of the great whales. It seems reasonable to assume that whales are likely to find it difficult to distinguish between the remnants of the mankind's industrial sounds and the sounds of other whales, and that these unnatural sounds might mask their calls and make it hard for them to understand each other and, perhaps, even find their way around.

Animals are generally good at adapting to environmental change, but only as long as it is neither too sudden nor too extreme. Recently, for instance, it has been discovered that dolphins seem to be able to turn down the sensitivity of their ears, but only in response to warning signals.

But there is more to man-made ocean noise than the sounds of oil exploration. There is also the noise from using the oil. When Leonardo Da Vinci put a long tube into the sea in 1490 he realised that the sound of ships (which in those days were, of course, sailing ships) carried for miles. Nowadays eighty per cent of the world's trade (by volume) is carried by sea in ships that are becoming ever larger and noisier. The largest container ships are thirteen hundred feet long, as long as the distance around an Olympic running track; their forty thousand horsepower engines drive twin, thirty-two feet wide, propellers at an average speed of twenty knots (about twenty two miles and hour); and make about one hundred and ninety decibels of sound, a sound that is the same intensity as a blue whale's low frequency song.

Of all man-made ocean noise the most continuous are ships propellers. Even small power boats can put out one hundred and sixty decibels. Container ships, war ships, cruise ships, ferries, fishing boats, icebreakers, submarines, tugs and pleasure boats - like yachts and ribs (rigid inflatable boats with outboard engines); they all add to the underwater noise levels that the water carries far and deep until they reverberate back from the ocean floor.

Add to the constant throb of ships' propellers the noise of ship's engines; the military's testing of high-powered sonar; the explosions from oil exploration (a two-pound explosion of TNT can carry about seven hundred miles); the scraping of trawlers as they dredge the ocean floor; the fishing tackle being winched up or let out; and you have a confused and complicated tangle of man-made disturbances.

Sudden noises like military sonar, the kind used to hunt submarines, seems to have a particularly violent effect. Often the disruption disturbs the whales' feeding. At worst, the animals flee in panic and end up stranded on shore. When that happens the chances of survival are slim, not least because without the buoyancy of water they are likely to be crushed by their own weight.

As the climate changes and more ice melts new shipping routes are opening up. Both the Northwest Passage, that connects the Pacific and the Atlantic Oceans, and the Northeast Passage, Russia's northern sea route from Murmansk to Thailand, have become free enough of ice to be used regularly now. The Chinese seem particularly intent on a 'polar Silk Road'. The proof is their 36,000-tonne ice-breaking cargo ship Tianen, built to withstand the harsh conditions. An Arctic channel cuts the distance between north east Asia and northern Europe by one third; cuts twelve days off the present route (via the Indian Ocean and the Suez Canal); and saves three hundred tonnes of fuel. Although this Arctic route will only be navigable in summer it seems likely that where the Chinese go others are bound to follow – follow across the Bering Sea and into the north Atlantic Ocean via the Bering Strait where whales are also summer visitors.

More shipping in more places means more noise and more ship strikes, the collisions between whales and shipping that take such a notorious toll they have become a principal threat to whale survival. And the larger and faster the ships, the more likely it is for whales to be struck and the more likely for strikes to go unnoticed. The great whales, like blues, fins, humpbacks and greys whose migration routes come near the west coast of North America's busy shipping lanes are particularly at risk. The US's Whale Alert network - whose main aim is to reduce ship strikes - have set up marine sanctuaries on both America's west and east coasts. The west coast sanctuaries encompass nearly thirteen thousand square miles where several endangered and threatened species have found they are reasonably safe from human interference. But only one per cent of the oceans are protected and there is no similar safe havens for whales in other main shipping areas like those around the Canary Islands; the north Indian Ocean; the Sea of Japan; or the principal sea route between Europe and India where the rare Arabian Sea humpbacks live among some of the world's busiest shipping lanes. For whales all over the planet the Oceans and Seas have become perilous places: one third of cetaceans found dead all over the world show signs of having been hit by a ship.

But mineral oil is needed for more than fuel to run noisy engines. It is also in demand to make the plastics that, like the sounds that reverberate all over the oceans, know no boundaries, and out of which the nets that snare sea animals are made.

Not everyone agrees with theories that man-made sounds are working against the interests of whales, especially those whose interests are oil interests. But what if the whales *are* being disturbed by man-made industrial sounds? What if these unnatural sounds are making it harder for whales to find food and locate each other? What if the sounds are disorientating enough to make it difficult for whales to navigate their migration routes? What will the consequences be then?

7

Taiji Mahal

"There are many great minds on earth and not all are human"
Anthony Douglas Williams

Mahal means a division, a share or portion, of a hunting ground. Taiji, off Japan's south east coast, is a small town. But it's hunting ground is vast - up to the horizon and far beyond.

Taiji's hunting season lasts for half the year, from September to April and dolphins are what Taiji's fishermen are after. The rewards are great. Live dolphins for a marine park fetch tens of thousands of US dollars, and dead dolphins, for meat, fetch hundreds. There is a lot at stake. Particularly for the dolphins.

Out in Taiji's bay Haruto and Toma were leading a forty-strong pod. These bottlenose dolphins are the largest bulls and the eldest in the herd. Haruto is in his early twenties and Toma is getting on for twenty-six. The other pod members like the way they are good at tracking down prey, so where the two big bulls go they follow. After all, Haruto and Toma have the experience. Experience that plays a great part in keeping them all safe.

Rio and Miya had been throwing seaweed at each other when the whistle went up. In no time at all the pod had formed itself into a line. Pushing forward at twelve miles an hour they porpoised along, rhythmically lifting themselves out of the water for less drag and a faster pace. The dolphins at the back fanned out and the pod began to form a loose circle. After they had forced the shoal they had been chasing into a bait ball – some can measure thirty feet in diameter - they took it in turns to dive down, charge through the fish, and feed. For about ninety seconds they gulped their prey down whole before going back to the surface for air and a very brief pause.

This chase had delivered sardines but it could have been herring, mackerel or any other schooling fish. But dolphins aren't fussy eaters: octopus, squid, crab, shrimps, even an occasional bird, are all part of their diet. But they do need to pack in the calories: sixty-six pounds a day for the fully grown, about five per cent of their body weight. And even more for nursing mothers.

They prefer hunting in water that isn't particularly deep, ideally not shallower than ten to twelve feet and no deeper than one hundred and fifty feet. Only rarely do they go down further or hold their breath for more than seven minutes. And sometimes they herd schools of fish against sand bars and mud banks, or chase them into the shallows where they flip them out of the water with their flukes. Another way of attracting fish is to slap their tails. For preference they hunt at night, but they are good at adapting if they have to, and they certainly don't like to miss an opportunity.

Co-operation over food is obviously useful and as a defence against predators safety in numbers is a good strategy too. When dolphins feel threatened they invariably take a stand. If a great white, or tiger or bull shark seem intent on approaching there are always some pod members who charge at the enemy intending to ram their snouts hard at the sharks' gills. Nearly always the would-be attacker leaves to look for easier prey. But not always. Several of the pod have scars from shark attacks. And then there are the ubiquitous orcas that roam over all oceans and are always on the lookout. Although orcas rarely attack a large pod they often try to separate mothers from calves, or pick on the weak or sick. All these animals are experienced killers – the dolphins, sharks and orcas – and there are lessons to be learnt from every encounter.

The newest mother in the pod is Namami. Mayu had weighed-in at a feminine thirty pounds and just over a meter in length. For this event experienced mothers Riko and Saka acted as midwives. They stroked and comforted Nanami until, when the baby was born, tail first, they helped to carry the new born Mayu, eyes open and fully alert, to the surface to take her first breath. Immediately all the other members of the pod, aware the blood from the birth might attract predators, had formed a circle round the mother and new baby, ready to fend off any unwelcome attention.

But for all the pod's confidence in Haruto's and Toma's ability to keep them safe, there was one predator they couldn't face off: humans. Against Taiji's fishermen they didn't stand a chance.

At first light twelve small boats set out. The drive hunt had begun. Some days the search is fruitless but most days it's not. And sometimes the fishermen don't even have to search.

To dolphins boats looked interesting and if anything looks as if it might be worth investigating they don't want to miss out. Inquisitive by nature anything novel - anything that might be edible or fun - and they feel compelled to find out more and almost invariably swim closer to check it out.

And this was where it all went wrong. Cruising along at a leisurely five miles an hour they came to the boat at the stern - their friendly approach, to show they came in peace. When they mean business, when aggression is called for, in defence or attack, they face their adversary full on with no holding back. But this time there seemed no call for that.

The moment they were spotted the boat that had made the sighting radioed the other crews. The first boat stayed where it was, until the other boats arrived and, in dolphin-like formation, formed a v-shaped wall around the inquisitive pod.

The dolphins were even more curious now, and just slightly anxious. But when the fishermen put lead pipes into the water and began to bang on them the ear shattering noise sent them into overwhelming confusion. It was pandemonium. They couldn't hear each other's individual whistles. They didn't know who was where. They didn't understand what was happening.

When, eventually, the sound stopped their feelings of terror did not. Their alarm calls fell on deaf ears as they were dragged along in a huge net, shoved together, jostled and pushed, and too close for comfort.

Eventually everything stopped and they found themselves cornered in an inlet. Taiji's infamous cove. A net was strung across its entrance. There was no hope of escape now, just as from the moment they were sighted there never had been. Imprisoned, trapped and petrified they could hardly move.

For a moment everything was eerily quite. Only then did they notice that Ichika looked as if she was in a bad way. She seemed too exhausted to breathe. But in the cramped space there was no room to help her. Mayu also seemed lifeless. Namami was frantic but being a good mother she tried not to show her panic and was nudging her and whistling to her gently. But her whistling turned into a groan. In all the turmoil Mayu had drowned. The confusion had so unnerved her that she had forgotten to breathe and in all the panic no-one had noticed. It had taken all their energy just to keep themselves going.

The quietness lasted only a few moments before people started wading in among them. They were trainers from a marine animal adventure park who had come to pick out the four young females they had ordered. Bottlenose dolphins are a favourite in dolphinarium shows and it is well known that Tajii is the place to find them. The trainers had come to pick out the most attractive animals, the ones that were still unblemished. And they preferred females who were more useful in breeding programmes. Since fully grown bottlenose dolphins can measure thirteen feet and weigh over one thousand pounds they take some manoeuvring , so the smaller and younger dolphins are what they are looking for. With thirty-eight surviving dolphins now penned in the cove, the buyers could take their pick at leisure.

All this time Rio had managed to stay close to Miya; since they were weaned they had been inseparable. When Rio saw Miya being lifted from the water he screamed and screamed and she screamed back. Yuna, Ichika and Natsuki had also been selected. Their pitiful cries and the cries of the pod carried far inland to where people were enjoying a fine evening out, seemingly oblivious to the distant clamour.

The four young dolphins were put in slings, hoisted onto a truck for transport to the airport. After the plane journey they will be put on another truck and be driven for several days until they arrive at Russia's largest dolphinarium, at Sochi on the Black Sea. Here the demand for dolphins is growing, as it is in other countries such as China, Ukraine, South Korea and Vietnam. The financial rewards are huge. This is a billion-dollar business. But for the animals it is a life of utter misery and unrelenting torture. But a humane movement is growing. All over the world there are places where marine parks have had to close when they fell out of favour as people realised the shows that were put on involved terrible suffering. In the UK, Chile, and Croatia; in Hungary Turkey, Israel and India; in Argentina and Australia's Queensland state, the pools that once held captive performing sea mammals are empty.

Ichika will not survive the journey - the stress of capture and the trauma of having been torn from her family will have been too much. At journey's end, and no less traumatised by all that has happened to them, Yuna and Natsuki will be put in a tank of chlorinated water where their whistles and clicks will bounce back from the concrete walls. They will be forced to perform silly tricks because to refuse is to go without food. In an attempt to keep them alive and from going mad their food will be medicated. Even so their lives will be short. In captivity records show that a performing dolphin's average lifespan is five years, hence the endless demand for replacements. In the wild they can live for forty years though fifteen to sixteen is average.

Eventually, in Taiji's cove, all went quiet and night fell. The remaining dolphins, those that had been rejected by the trainers and were destined to become meat, were beyond giving each other any form of comfort. All in despair and utterly wretched during that long, interminable night - night when, normally, if things were as they should have been, they would have been out hunting, covering miles of ocean, as free as birds in the air.

With dawn came a host of unfamiliar noises, human noises: loud voices, clattering, scraping and hard, metallic unfamiliar sounds. A long drawn-out rustling sound brought darkness. A tarpaulin had been spread out over them.

And then the slaughter began. They were taken one at a time. Shota was the first to be selected. A metal pin was rammed into his neck, just below his blowhole. His scream was blood curdling. Fear and pain and shock, all in one. Systematically the killers worked their way through the pod. Death was slow and the suffering was obvious as they writhed and groaned in pain while those waiting their fate, found their teeth chattered uncontrollably and the whites of their eyes made a ghastly spectral contrast to the blood that was everywhere: the water was red, their skin was red, and their killers were streaked with red.

At one time the Taiji fishermen used to slit the dolphins throats so that they bled to death. Death then was relatively quick but even more bloody. Now, so that the bleeding will be less, this new method is used, a method that is slow, excruciating painful and unfathomably brutal and makes death slower, often six, eight or even fifteen minutes slower. The official version claims that the dolphins die in seconds even though, in recognition of the cruelty it inflicts, the Japanese have made it unlawful to kill cows this way. But the Taiji fishermen and dolphin butchers carry on regardless, seemingly unaffected by the blood and the fear and the carnage they are wreaking.

Eventually all is quiet and the dead are taken to the butcher house.

And all a consequence of humans' cavalier attitude to the feelings of other species.

8

Faecal Matters

*"For most of history, man has had to fight nature to
survive; in this century he is beginning to realize that,
in order to survive, he must protect it."*
Jacques-Yves Cousteau, Oceanographer

Buniq is a bowhead whale. Like all bowheads her home is in
the most northern waters of the northern hemisphere. This is the
Arctic, the polar opposite to the Antarctic, but not just for being
at the opposite ends of Earth. In the southernmost polar region
Antarctica - the highest, driest, and most windy continent on
Earth – is surrounded by ocean, whereas the Arctic, Earth's
most northern polar region, is not a continent but an ice-covered
ocean surrounded by land.

For the northernmost whales - the narwhals, belugas and
bowheads - the Arctic is their permanent home, a place they
never leave. Even in winter, when temperatures can drop to −50
°C, they venture no further south than where the pack ice ends.
But the Arctic whales are not the only animals who winter here.
There are also ice seals, so-called because they live on the ice:
the bearded, ribbon, ringed, spotted, harp and hooded seals.
With krill in abundance and two hundred and forty species of
fish the feeding is good.

Here in the north, where in mid-summer it is perpetually light
and in mid-winter perpetually dark, the water is always
freezing. For warmth Buniq has the thickest blubber of any
animal, about one and half foot thick. As a result she is a whale
of great rotundity and impressive size; and, like most female
baleen whales, larger than most males. Her length is sixty foot

and her weight fifty-four tons. Her deeply notched triangular flukes are twenty-five feet from tip to tip and her wide, paddle-shaped flippers six feet long. She has no distinct neck and her head, being one third of her body length, is of extreme amplitude. Also of immense dimensions is her hugely arched ten foot wide upper jaw which is the shape of an Inuit hunting bow after which bowheads are named. Her mouth is twenty foot deep, and the largest mouth on Earth. Her lifespan of over two hundred years is only equalled by the slow growing Greenland Shark (four hundred years is its highest reported age)and the Ocean Quahog clam (whose oldest reported age is five hundred and seven years). Like the Greenland Shark Buniq is also a slow developer. She will not reach her reproductive age until she is twenty five; and not be fully grown until she is between forty to fifty years old.

For Buniq feeding is a serious business and, since she needs two tons of food a day, feeding is how she spends most of her time. With her cavernous mouth wide open, she glides through the water at between one to two and a half miles an hour, scooping up zooplankton, that is mostly krill and copepods. Her annual intake of these tiny crustaceans is about one hundred tons a year. As she takes in her feed she presses her one ton tongue against the roof of her mouth to expel the water and, through three hundred and fifty pairs of overlapping black baleen plates, sieves her prey

The largest of her baleen plates are fourteen feet long and nearly one foot wide, all edged with silver-coloured bristles. Just as no whale has a mouth that is larger no whales have baleens that are longer. But she is not the speediest of whales. Cruising at two to seven miles and hour might be a typical whale speed but a top speed of ten to twelve miles an hour, and only then if pushed, is not, which makes her the slowest of whales. Bowheads are built for warmth, not haste.

Buniq often feeds with Kassuq and Tartok. Sometimes their dives last no more than four minutes, other times they might take twenty; but they rarely dive for more than an hour or deeper than two hundred metres. And often they feed below the ice. When they need to come up to breathe they use their vast skulls and the great power of their bodies to break through and shatter the ice – ice that might be two feet thick - to make breathing holes. And then they spout their v-shaped spumes twenty feet up into the freezing Arctic air, where the Arctic winds often roar and storms frequently rage.

In the still waters below you might expect there to be an eerie quietness. But the sounds that resound off the ice above and the seabed below are as rich and varied as in any other ocean. During the long dark winter the low frequency haunting songs of bowheads pass endlessly between each other, a sound that can carry for hundreds of miles. Their chorus is rich and loud and varies according to their clan, age and sex. Some are simple moans, some are complex pulses and some imitate others' songs exactly. As their calls reverberate through the icy water they help the whales navigate the darkness and let others know where each whale is.

The narwhals - the so-called unicorns of the sea for their long spiral tusks - make their presence felt too. Their whistles, squeals, trills, and knocking and trumpeting sounds resound through the water. Their clicks and squeaks are probably for echolocation, for plotting their course and hunting their prey that is, mostly, Arctic cod and Greenland halibut.

The songs of the belugas' - the small white toothed whales – have higher tones. When they group together they sound like human children in a play ground, and their songs are so melodic that they are also known as the canaries of the sea.

But there are more than whale songs to be heard underneath the ice. The seals mid-frequency tones rise and fall as they call to each other. The swish of large fish shoals carry for miles. And, when the weather is still, the padding of polar bears resounds through the ice as do the adult bears' chuffs, hisses, snorts and growls and their cubs' higher-pitched hums, groans and cries.

In summer, when other whales come to feed here, their songs are added to the mix: the low frequency booming of humpbacks, greys, finbacks, seis and northern minkes; and the sharp tuneful sounds of killer whales, the only dolphin that can tolerate the cold Arctic waters.

But it is not just the tones of marine animals that resonate under the ice. The ice itself has a whole range of acoustics – particularly in winter. The polar sea ice – that can freeze one inch an hour;, one foot in two days, and is on average three to six feet thick and at its thickest fifteen feet - is not like the ice of frozen rivers. It's in a state of impermanence. The ice-cap is crossed with crevasses and cracks. As ice-storms with winds - that can reach over one hundred miles an hour - howl and scream they carry shards of clattering ice that form hummocks several feet high and ridges that rise up tens of feet. The pack, or drift ice - the great expanses of sections of floating ice- also has its own sound effects. As these ice floes shift with the waves they grind against each other, and when storms lift them up, crack and bang as they break into smaller pieces. Glaciers are also perpetually on the move, though at a ponderous pace; about three feet a day is typical. When calving glaciers break off and fall into the Ocean the sounds of their splitting are as loud and resounding as any gunshot. But the loudest sound of all the Arctic's natural sounds, and one of the loudest ever recorded, is the clash of colliding icebergs. It seems the animals know what they are as they don't seemed disturbed by them at all.

Sometimes the bowheads skim the surface to feed and then their dark skin, triangular heads and smooth, rounded backs make a clear contrast to the ice around them. Groups of three to six are not unusual but when they head north in the spring they sometimes join together in groups of fifty.

But bowhead numbers are not as great as they once were. From the beginning of the seventeenth century until well into the twentieth they were hunted in earnest. Now their population seems to be between eight and twelve thousand, down from an estimated fifty thousand in pre-whaling days. But in the Sea of Okhotsk there are only about one hundred and fifty - or perhaps two hundred – left. Even so, the indigenous Canadians and Russians still hunt them.

The eighteen foot Belugas are probably in hundreds of thousands, even though they too were hunted for centuries, for their meat, blubber and skin - they are only cetacean whose skin is thick enough to use as leather. But today their value lies in their performance in marine parks.

As for the number of the rarely seen twelve to twenty foot narwhals; that is impossible to estimate.

After a few short blows Buniq arches her back, up and out of the water, and with her flukes hardly breaking the surface, she begins to dive. A pink cloud forms behind her: her faecal matter. This is a substance of fundamental significance for the part it plays in the oceans' cycles of disposal and renewal, and for its crucial place in the Arctic Ocean's ecosystem.

This waste product - urine and faeces mixed together - is only loosely solid and Buniq's daily output is equivalent to three per cent of her body mass. The colour varies through many shades of pink, from reddish to vibrant orange depending on what she has eaten. And what she has eaten is, usually, zooplankton that include the ubiquitous but diminutively sized krill; the larvae of fish and squid; and also other tiny crustaceans that are small enough to filter through her baleens

The bowheads' colourful waste is deposited close enough to the surface for a faecal and solar symbiosis to take place. Just as the whales need krill to feed on, so the krill needs to feed, and what they feed on are phytoplankton, microscopic, plant-like, micro algae. But like plants on land these diminutive floating plants cannot exist without sunlight. They need to photosynthesise, to absorb the sun' s light for energy to convert carbon dioxide and minerals - that include iron from the whales' faecal deposit - into carbohydrates; then, having taken as many carbohydrates as they need to grow, expel those they don't as oxygen.

And so phytoplankton - the feed of zooplankton that are the feed of the great baleen whales - wax and wane according to the seasons, the number of daylight hours and the nutrients available - nutrients that includes the whales' iron-rich faecal matter. They can cluster in vast blooms one hundred of yards thick, or merely form a surface layer.

If measured by mass iron is Earth's most common element. Most is in Earth's outer and inner cores, but it is also exists in the atmosphere and in seawater, originating from, among other things, volcanic ash and hot springs on the ocean floor. But it is not evenly spread and areas that are deficient in iron are short of plankton too – which makes the whales' iron-rich, peripatetic, waste product a crucial nutrient in the plankton's ability to thrive.

In turn, plankton's waste product, is oxygen – Earth's most common element when measured by volume - and the whales' gas of life. Together – the iron and the oxygen - form a life-giving, virtuous cycle: a fusion of sunlight and minerals that form an indispensable, interdependent relationship which all creatures depend on, from those of the greatest size to the tiniest and microscopic. This is a cycle that keeps nature in balance, where phytoplankton feed zooplankton that feed the fish that feed the seals that polar bears feed on. And when whales return to the surface and their digestion - which closes down during very deep dives - begins to work again their faecal output enters that fundamental cycle of all living things. Only for those female whales, who in the breeding season eat almost nothing at all, is there a pause in faecal production as fasting whales do not defecate.

Like all fish and all the other marine animals that need oxygen to breathe, when whales breathe, defecate and break wind they make a contribution to the ocean's carbon dioxide content. But it has been calculated that when they deposit their faecal matter they make up for their CO_2 emissions by a factor of two because plankton, by benefiting from the whales' faeces, absorb twice as much carbon dioxide as the whales emitted in the first place.

And so Earth's eighty-six species of cetaceans, in all their various sizes and types, contribute to the nutrient balance of life: the six porpoise species; the forty types of dolphins, from the largest who are orcas to the smallest Maui's dolphins that weigh just about one hundred pounds and are not much more than a metre long even when fully grown. And, of course, all the great whales: the eleven species of baleen whales and the great toothed whales: the sperm whales, belugas, narwhals and beaked whales. All those, along with every one of the Earth's other animals and micro-organisms, playing their part in the natural cycling of organic materials, including plankton that plays such a vital part at the basis of the oceanic food web.

The importance of plankton on which so much marine life depends cannot be underestimated; it's the reason these drifting plants are regarded as indicators of the health of the oceans' ecosystems - systems that could so easily be put out of balance in the event of a faecal deficit.

9

Consequences

"The Law of unintended consequence is the real law of history."

Niall Ferguson
British historian and political commentator

In the old parlour game 'Consequences' the first player writes a sentence to describe someone, and then hides what they wrote by folding the paper over. The next player writes who that person might be, and folds the paper over. As the paper is passed round the third player describes another person; the fourth names the person just described; the fifth tells where the two people met; the sixth what the first person gave the second person; the seventh tells what the first person said to the second person; the eighth player writes the second person's reply; the ninth player describes the consequences; and, finally, the last player writes what the world said about it.

So, for example, the game could go like this.

> (1) The dishevelled and beleaguered (2) naturalist, Sir David Attenborough (3) met the intrepid and esteemed (4) beaked whale (5) in the Bay of Mexico. (6) He gave her an overcoat made from fishing nets (7) and she said "the sea is a universal sewer". (8) He replied "the race for oxygen is on" (9) and the consequence is that there is nothing in the sea but plastic and jellyfish. And the world said (10) "Some people create their own storms then get upset when it rains."

If you want fun mixed with surrealism this is a good game. But the difference with this example is that it is far from fanciful. For whales, and for all marine life, the descriptions are perilously close to the consequences of humans' impact on the marine world.

And the world said "I said to my reflection, let's get out of this place"

Joe Cocker Lyrics *Tempted*

Every year about six hundred cetaceans are washed up on the UK's coast line. Most are dolphins and porpoises, including killer and pilot whales who are, taxonomically, oceanic dolphins, and the largest and second largest of their kind. But great whales wash up too: on average, five a month. The most usual casualties are toothed whales, such as sperm and beaked whales.

There is no shortage of speculation as to why these great animals wash up on the world's shores, but the actual causes are seldom so clear. The circumstances could be natural, or they could be the consequences of human activity.

Some of the animals might have died from from old age or ill health. They could have died far away and been carried ashore by the winds and the tides. Or had they still been alive when they found themselves stranded, and drowned when the tide came in and covered their blowholes? Might they have been pushed off course by severe storms? Or had their food source been brought perilously close to land by a change in ocean currents? Perhaps they made navigation errors? Might they have been confused by solar storms? This is something NASA (the National Aeronautics and Space Administration) are currently researching: whether explosions in the Sun's atmosphere could upset the whales' navigation. Or could the whales have become disorientated and lost their bearings when they found themselves in the relatively shallow waters of the continental shelf? Since the whales that are most commonly washed up tend to be deep divers – like sperm and beaked whales who live far out in the ocean- this last seems a plausible explanation

In 2014 the UK's count of beached whales included nineteen long-finned pilot whales; fifteen minkes; one humpback; eight Cuvier's beaked whales; four Sowerby's beaked whales; seven sperm whales; one beluga whale; one orca; and two pygmy sperm whales.

Pygmy sperm whales are rarely sighted at sea so most of the very little that is known about them has to be deduced from those that wash up on beaches. Compared to a fifty to sixty foot, fifty-six ton, bull sperm whale, being eleven and a half feet long and less than half a ton makes 'pygmy' an apt description. Though at nine feet, dwarf sperm whales, who are more often seen at sea, are smaller still and the smallest of all whales, even smaller than the larger dolphins. Only one baleen whale, the right whale, has a pygmy relation though only in name. In reality this whale is a separate species. Until 2012 pygmy right whales were thought to have been extinct for two million years. Measuring eighteen feet they are the smallest of all baleen whales, though easily mistaken for minkes and are exclusive to the southern hemisphere, where more have been found stranded than seen alive.

Sometimes cetaceans beach themselves in large groups, a calamity that is often taken as evidence of the strength of a pod's social structure. Since pods that have strong bonds tend to follow a leader, as dolphins do - including pilot whales and hence their name - perhaps this is a reasonable conclusion. That was the theory when one hundred false killer whales died after stranding themselves on Florida's Highland Beach in January 2017. It was supposed that the pod had been following a sick member who was heading for shallow water to avoid drowning.

In November 2018, on New Zealand's remote Stewart Island (nearly twenty miles south of South Island) there was a mass standing of one one hundred and forty-five pilot whales. The same week twelve pygmy killer whales were found stranded, on the north-west of North Island, on Ninety Mile Beach. Nearby, on Doubtless Bay, a sperm whale had washed up; and, also on the west coast, a female pygmy sperm whale.

Although pilot whales are quite often found stranded on New Zealand's beaches during the summer, other types of whale usually aren't. That a cluster of strandings happened in a very short time raises several questions. Were these animals sick? Or might they have been escaping a predator? Had they been caught out by a rapidly falling tide? Or was extreme weather the cause? At the time of the strandings New Zealand's ocean temperatures were the warmest ever recorded. Could it be that an increase in ocean temperature had affected the whales' behaviour?

And what is the explanation for the largest mass stranding ever recorded? In 2017, in Golden Bay, near the northern tip of New Zealand's South Island, six hundred and fifty-six pilot whales beached themselves. Two hundred managed to refloat; three hundred and fifty-five died; and the few that were still alive were helped back to the sea by volunteers. But whether these third largest of dolphins (that can weigh over two tons and whose average length is sixteen feet) survived their trauma is unknown.

If it had been great whales rather than dolphins that had been helped back to the sea after beaching their survival would have been unlikely. Without water to support their enormous bulk the pressure of their weight would have damaged internal organs and muscles. The injured muscles would have released myoglobin (an iron and oxygen-binding protein that is the muscles' main oxygen-carrier) and the blood would have carried the protein to the kidneys. Once there it would have caused acute injury, kidney failure and certain death. Being returned to the water cannot save a great whale because then the blood circulates more freely and the lethal myoglobin reaches the kidneys even more quickly.

No doubt some strandings can be blamed on human activities, but, like the explanations based on natural circumstances, they too are often more conjecture than proof.

And the world said "If we amplify everything we hear nothing."

Jon Stewart, American actor and comedian 2010

Man-made sounds are high on the long list of human intrusions into the whales' world. What is certain is that the oceans' are becoming increasingly industrialised and wherever there is industry there is noise - unnatural sounds that are likely interfere with cetaceans' biosonar, their biological echolocation systems.

From coasts and offshore developments there is the perpetual din of industry. From the construction of oil and gas installations the thumping of pile drivers. From the oil industry, drilling and fracking. From the military, high-intensity sonar tests. From offshore wind farms the turning of wind turbines. From shipping, fishing vessels and pleasure craft the throb of engines and propellers. From holiday resorts jet skis that sound like a high speed race, a sound that in water – like all sounds - is louder and travels faster and further. Even the sounds of aircraft overhead reverberate through the oceans' waters.

The sounds sent out by pile drivers can register from eighty to one hundred and fifty decibels. At the top end of those figures the eardrums of humans can burst; swim bladders of fish can rupture; and the hearing of whales can be damaged- which for animals like toothed cetaceans who rely on sound to navigate, is, in effect, a death sentence.

Since the 1990s eighty-two sperm whales have been found stranded on the beaches of the Wadden Sea (the south eastern part of the North Sea, bordered by Denmark, the Netherlands and Germany). Why weren't these whales where they usually are, far out in the deep, north Atlantic? What made them come to these relatively shallow waters? Could their deaths be a consequence of man-made industrial sounds? It's hard to tell.

In 2017 an international conference (titled *Towards an Acoustically Sound Ocean*) was held in Barcelona. Experts reported on models, demonstrated with maps, made suggestions for regulations and procedures, and debated the cost of mitigating man-made sounds in the oceans. But discussing what should - or ought - to be done is not the same as doing it.

We cannot not be sure of the extent that man-made sounds affect marine life. And neither does it seem likely that we could turn those unnatural noises down even if we wanted to.

And the world said "Water and air, the two essential fluids on which all life depends, have become global garbage cans."

Oceanographer Jacques-Yves Cousteau

The first industrial impact on the oceans was made by whaling. But since mineral oil replaced whale oil, and plastic replaced whalebone, and commercial whaling was banned, some of the great whale populations are making a comeback from the three centuries of industrial-scale whaling that decimated their forebears.

But now the whales have new hazards to contend with. The consequence of prospecting for fossil fuels, and their mining and fracking have polluted great tracts of continental shelves with oil spills, toxic chemicals, noise and vibrations. Add to that pollution from coastal industry, the runoff from agriculture, and all the other noxious by-products of human activity, and the whales environment begins to look precarious. But it's not always easy to tell.

Worldwide the great whales might number about two million, though probably less. Those who wash up on beaches are just a tiny fraction of that number which means that the marine biologists who study their lives and deaths don't have a lot to go on. But it is clear that marine pollution is a major problem and the development of coastal industries a major factor in damaging their ocean habitats, often with catastrophic and, sometimes, unique consequences.

Off Argentina's Patagonian nature reserve on Peninsula Valdes the southern right whales have a particular problem. Human effluent and waste from landfills has increased and the kelp gull population, attracted by such bounty, has grown larger. The whales' dilemma is that the gulls have also developed a taste for the skin and blubber of very young calves. Since newborn whales need to breathe every few minutes the gulls have plenty of opportunity to attack and often peck at calves every time they come to the surface. That they inflict painful wounds is obvious. But the attacks can last for hours, exhausting and weakening calves that should be using their energy to grow. Their loss of stamina puts them in mortal danger and the number of dead calves is increasing. But only half of the calves who die have gull inflicted wounds, and so it seems the reason for their deaths is not as clear as it first appears.

On southern Africa's western coast Namibia's coastline is abundant with wild life. Endangered sea birds, like the African Penguin and the Cape Gannet, come to breed on the offshore islands and islets. Here too, at Walvis Bay, is southern Africa's most important coastal wetland for migrating birds. Other frequent visitors include twenty-three types of dolphin and eight species of baleen whales. But even in this wildlife haven the consequences of human activity have made their mark.

When Portuguese mariners arrived at the bay in the sixteenth century they were so astonished by the huge number of whales they named it Bahia das Bahleas: the Bay of Whales. And then, when the first commercial whalers arrived – sent by the Dutch West India Company in 1726 - they changed the name to Walvisch Baye, hence walvis, a corruption of 'walvisch', Dutch for whale. By 1780 the Dutch had been joined by French and Norwegian whalers. Now Namibia's Skeleton Coast is named for its bleached whale bones - testament to the success of the whaling industry: the whalers had hunted the southern right and humpback whales to the point of extinction. By the mid1960s they had all but been wiped out.

But now, thanks to the ban on commercial whaling in1986, southern right whales and humpbacks are being spotted again.

They are back where the upwelling of the cold Benguela Current brings up the nutrients that plankton thrive on. A rich feeding ground, ideal for whales, and a lucrative hunting territory for commercial fisheries.

But Namibia's once pristine coastal waters are no longer as healthy as they were in the days when whale bones were piling up on the Skeleton Coast. Over the last two decades all manner of industrial development has spread along the coast. Sewage treatment facilities, fish processing plants, desalination projects, oil platforms. Construction of all kinds continues apace.

More industry means more noise; more chemical effluent; more water pollution; and, with the expansion of Namport's container terminal, more shipping traffic. Oil pollution is now a major factor in this part of the South Atlantic Ocean. And in the Gulf of Mexico there is a similar story.

Seventy miles off Florida's west coast the number of Brydes whales has fallen so low they are at risk of being unable to recover. Estimates on their number vary from fewer than one hundred to less than fifteen to thirty. To make a serious matter even more serious, these critically endangered whales have a unique feature among Bryde's: they are a sub species, which means their gene pools are so different they could never breed with any others.

These Bryde's do indeed seem doomed in these industrialised waters. Ship strikes are an ongoing hazard. There is the constant noise from shipping; the spasmodic uproar from military testing and training; from the oil and gas industries the sounds of siesmic guns and drilling, and also, from oil exploration and refining, oil leakages and, at worst, oil spills.

When BP's Deep Horizon oil-rig exploded in 2010 in the Gulf of Mexico, nearly half of the Bryde's whales' habitat was slicked. It was the largest oil spill in US history. For eighty-seven days millions of barrels of oil discharged into the sea. Some was recovered, some was burned, but thirty per cent could not be unaccounted for. Although most habitats recover naturally from oil spills it takes time, and the deeper oil lies the longer it takes to clear. Marine research scientists are debating whether oil from the Deep Horizon explosion could have sunk to the ocean floor and be harming an even greater area than they first thought. What is certain is that the Gulf's deep-sea corals have been affected, which at the bottom of the food web cannot but have consequences for a myriad of life above.

A slick's initial affects are more obvious, and animals coated in oil a familiar image. But it's more than being covered in oil that harms them. Crude oil floating on the surface is itself a toxic mixture of chemicals that release noxious fumes, and the chemicals that are used to clean up the oil compound the harmful affect. Some of these chemicals are cytotoxic, which means they are harmful to cells and a potential cause of skin irritations, liver disease and respiratory complications such as pneumonia. Others are genotoxic: potential disruptors of gene function and a cause of mutations that can be passed to the next generation, and also a possible cause of reproductive problems. Two years after the Deep Horizon disaster three-quarters of the pregnant bottlenose dolphins in the slick's area failed to give birth to a live calf. Nevertheless new deep water drilling permits have been approved in this area. In 2019, after discovering that an existing oilfield held one billion more barrels than they expected, BP announced plans to increase its oil production by one third (thus putting this British international oil and gas company top of the list of the Gulf of Mexico's biggest oil producers).

No-one knows how the spill has affected the Gulf's Bryde's whales, nor the Gulf 's other endangered whales, the blue, finback, humpback, sei and sperm whales. Could oil on baleen plates make capturing prey less effective? Research on this is in progress. As for the effect of toxic chemicals. As with so much research into whales, data deficiency - a lack of evidence - abounds.

A disaster like the Deep Horizon's makes it seem as if oil and gas extraction is the oceans' main source of oil pollution. But this is not the case. If oil pollution is assessed on a global scale the proportion caused by offshore drilling is tiny – about two per cent - compared with other sources. Most - thirty-seven per cent - comes from the land, from the improper and unthinking disposal of engine oil into drains, and from street run off from motor vehicles. Nineteen percent is caused by the routine maintenance of ships. Thirteen per cent comes from air pollution (from hydrocarbons that fall as acid rain); ten per cent is natural seepage (that leaks through fractures in the seafloor); and five per cent is caused by oil tanker spills.

Unlike oil, a large number of the oceans' toxic pollutants are not so conspicuous. Heavy metals are some of them. Although metals occur naturally in the oceans, industrial activity has added to their mass and their effect on marine life can be lethal. Corals are particularly vulnerable as they are exceptionally efficient at absorbing them. In an attempt to diminish their impact synthetic reefs are being constructed. Coated in aluminium oxide they have been designed to absorb traces of potentially lethal metallic elements from the water. But heavy metals, since they originate from the Earth's crust, can never be destroyed. Usually their impact on most sea-life is not as severe as it is on corals. But heavy metal contamination can, over time, weaken immune systems and lower breeding rates.

The list of toxic elements that are used in all kinds of industrial activity (from agriculture to pharmaceuticals, from sewage to paint) is long. In theory some can be removed from sediments or covered up, like the now banned, or at least restricted, man-made PCBs. But like plastics they too are everywhere and were designed to last.

Given the nature of chemical pollution and the size of the oceans, the toxic chemical problem seems to be similar to plastics. It's on a vast and, mostly, non-eradicable scale.

And the world said "If you have seen an entangled marine mammal please click the button below to fill out a form with the details of entanglement."
Australian Marine Mammal Centre

Every year, all over the world, hundreds of thousands of animals are killed when they get caught up in commercial fishing gear and other kinds of plastic debris.

The great whales are no exception. Even very large fins and flukes are no defence. They get caught in fixed and free-floating nets, and by long lines set on the surface and on the ocean floor. They get snagged in ropes fixed to crab and lobster pots, and most of all, in nets and lines that are lost or discarded. Abandoned fishing gear is in all the oceans, at all depths, and it's on beaches everywhere both on, and beneath, the sand.

But there's more than fishing equipment that entangles even the largest marine animals. The assortment of man-made marine paraphernalia that can enmesh them is vast. Some whales get attached to buoys, or the ubiquitous plastic strapping that is used for packaging, or are snagged by cables. In 2018, off Hawaii, rescuers cut free a humpback who was caught up in two hundred and eighty five foot of rope. For smaller animals six pack holders are a particular hazard; but anything that is looped, like scraps of fishing nets, plastic bags – even lavatory seats and Frisbees - snare heads and feet.

The effects of being entangled are dire: starvation, infection or death, usually from drowning, or, with a whale's ability to move away from marine traffic compromised, vessel strikes. Research has shown that seventy-eight per cent of right whales and sixty-six per cent of humpbacks that pass along North America's east coast had become entangled at least once in their lives, some several times; and calves more often than the adults, though why that should be is still a mystery.

Globally the toll is massive. Estimations are that fishing gear - that litters all the oceans - entangles at least three hundred thousand cetaceans every year. But more still are killed by the plethora of other marine debris, a number that is impossible to calculate.

And the world said "Ship strikes are more common than you might think"

Business Insider 2014

When whales find their way into busy shipping lanes they find themselves in particular jeopardy. Collisions with vessels often go unreported and, when animals are struck by the largest ships, even unnoticed. Sometimes ships come into port completely unaware they have a whale carcase draped over their bow.

For whales the hazards keep mounting. Ninety per cent of all the goods that are moved across the world are transported by sea, and ships are getting bigger, faster and carrying more cargo on more routes. The oceans, that were once exclusively highways for whales, have become through-routes for marine traffic: for container ships, oil carriers, car transporters, fish processing vessels, ferries, cruise liners and pleasure boats.

If whales are beached after being struck by a ship the evidence is usually clear. Broken skulls and open, sometimes festering, wounds, especially where they have been slashed by a propeller, are the proof. But how many die out in the ocean? The estimated numbers of marine animals that are killed by ship strikes can never be accurate.

And the world said "The Hell with Everything. Let's Get Rich."

All the Trouble in the World. P.J. O'Rourke 1994

Fish stocks all over the world are being depleted at such alarming levels that seventy per cent of all the fish we use - to feed not only ourselves and but also our farm animals, including farmed fish - have already been taken, or so say some marine ecologists. But others maintain these claims are exaggerated and that the proportion of fish stocks that are over-exploited are, at most, thirty-three per cent, and the amount of fish populations that have collapsed, thirteen per cent.

The research might be rigorous but, as these conflicting figures show, that does not make them accurate, particularly when so many figures are based on assumptions. Even legitimate global fishing fleets take more fish than they report. Foreign vessels disregard the laws of other states and fail to declare catches above the permitted tonnage. Add to that the illegal side of fishing, a black-market where laws are treated with disdain and nothing is licensed. Being unreported, unregulated and unmanaged, the destruction caused by illicit fishing is as difficult to assess as it is to police. But in spite of that reckonings have been made: unlawful fishing could be taking between fourteen and thirty-three per cent of all fish caught.

And then, to compound the harm, there are destructive and illegal fishing methods, like those that use poison and explosives. Cyanide kills not only the intended catch but decimates countless flora and fauna. Blast fishing, with dynamite or home made bombs, has the same, indiscriminate effect. Both devastate ecosystems, particularly coral reefs which are a favoured target - reefs that, although they cover just one percent of the ocean floor, support about a quarter of all marine life. Half the world's tropical coral reefs are said to be at risk of overfishing, and almost all of South East Asia's.

But not all destructive methods are illegal. Bottom trawling by lawful commercial fisheries - to catch ground fish like cod, shrimp and squid - destroys entire seabed environments, including corals, and stirs up plumes of sediment so vast they can be seen from space: every year an area of seafloor twice the size of the United States of America.

Lost fishing equipment is no less damaging as abandoned gear entangles an unknown number of animals and forgotten drift nets meander aimlessly for years continuing to fish and trap all manner of creatures. Add to that the wastage of unintentional, unwanted and discarded parts of a catch, known as bycatch. Bycatch might include turtles, seabirds, sharks and whales and it applies to the legal trade as much as it does to illegal fishing. This unintended catch of the unprofitable or unpalatable, or the too young or too small, is reckoned to represent forty-percent of the world's wild-caught seafood.

Combine bycatch with overfishing and destructive fishing methods and the consequences are likely to be the depletion of fish stocks beyond their ability to recover - or in other words an unsustainable situation, a situation that cannot be maintained at the current level – and means that if we continue fishing at the present rate all the species we regard as seafood could be wiped out.

But the results of overfishing have far more serious consequences than a dearth of sea food for humans and farm animals. The knock-on affects of any shift in an ocean ecosystem can be acutely serious. Taking out just one species can have a disastrous affect for animals that depend on the food chain below, or above.

For instance, overfish the fish that feed the squid that feed the seals that orcas feed on. Then seals go hungry, their numbers go down, and orcas look for other types of food such as sea otters. Then there are fewer otters. But otters eat the sea urchins that eat the kelp. With nothing to keep the sea urchins in check they decimate the kelp forests. Yet hundreds of species – like snails, crabs, shrimps, fish and seabirds - depend on kelp forests for food and shelter,.

But nature usually has a way of sorting things out. So when the sea urchins have eaten nearly all the kelp their numbers plummet and the kelp recovers.

But that's the natural world. The impact of humans can be far more devastating. The human attitude "if I don't take it someone else will" is the premise of the economic theory known as 'the tragedy of the commons'. Commercial fishing is a perfect example. It's said that the number of fish stocks that face collapse has doubled in the last twenty years. But despite warnings, factory ships get bigger, take ever more fish, and fish stocks become more imperilled still.

But even subsistence fishermen (who fish not for sport but for their families and relatives) can have devastating effects on the areas they rely on for fish. One quarter of the world's small-scale fisherman rely on tropical coral reefs for their main food supply, reefs that are home to one-third of all fish species and support a greater variety of life than a tropical rainforest.

The reefs are formed from flower-like marine invertebrates, brilliantly coloured polyps, whose calcareous, chalky, hard, skeletons form their basis. Corals can only grow and thrive if they have a source of calcium carbonate, a vital chemical compound that is provided in part by rock-hard, calcareous, red algae. By binding together the dead coral skeletons the algae keeps reefs stable, and also provide a seedbed for young corals to grow - corals whose skeletons will in turn, after a lifespan of a couple of years, combine with those that have been building up - thin layer upon thin layer of calcium carbonate - over thousands of years (between five thousand to ten thousand years is a reef's typical lifespan).

These are delicate ecosystems where every form of life is food for another; where the corals live on plankton and tiny algal cells (that live inside them) that, in turn, support many other types of algae; where the algae are grazed by herbivores that are eaten by the smaller carnivorous fish; and the smaller fish are eaten by bigger fish until, at the top of the food chain, the largest predators, like goliath groupers, sharks and some toothed whales, eat them.

The reefs' stability is vital for an immense variety of life, from sponges to molluscs - such as snails, clams, sea slugs, oysters, octopus and squid; and echinoderms like starfish, urchins and sea cucumbers; and crustaceans from tiny planktonic copepods to lobsters and crabs; and eels, sea snakes, sea turtles and sea horses (there are fifty four species of these marine fish). And whales, dolphins and birds are among those who come to enjoy the reefs' abundance are. No wonder Charles Darwin compared coral reefs to oases in the desert.

On Kenya's coral reefs the sea urchin population is kept in check by their main predators, triggerfish and wrasse. When these were overfished the natural predator-prey balance up was upset: without the predators there was nothing to control sea urchin numbers. And so the reefs became over-grazed, their structure weakened, and the habitat for a host of marine animals was devastated - including fish for Kenya's small-scale fishermen.

But devastation could have happened another way. If too many herbivores had been taken the ungrazed reefs would have become overgrown and smothered the algae and coral – a situation that shows that all members of the food web, whether at the top or the bottom, play an equally vital part in keeping the reefs' delicate ecosystem in balance

Over the last one hundred years Earth's large prey fish have declined by two thirds, including the large sharks. Every year one hundred million are killed - eleven thousand every hour, or so the reckoning goes - mainly to supply the Asian market with shark fins and meat. In the north west Atlantic the shark population is heading for extinction and with their main predators gone there have been unsuspected consequences: a huge increase in smaller sharks, rays, and skates. Their escalation has led to the decimation of North Carolina's scallop, oyster and clam fisheries, a loss that not only affects those who enjoy eating shellfish but alters the quality of the water. Without the filter feeding shellfish there is nothing to filter microscopic particles from the water and keep it clean.

Large sharks also play an important part in keeping the oceans healthy. As quick dispatchers of animals that are sick or weak, and as scavengers of carcasses - including dead whales - they help prevent, or at least slow, the spread of infectious diseases. They also make a contribution to putting the brakes on global warming. As they pass over seagrass meadows, where their mere presence scares off animals like sea cows and turtles, they help prevent the overgrazing of these important carbon sinks. For seagrasses are more than just fodder for the oceans' grazers: they absorb twice as much carbon dioxide as forests on land. Although just 0.2 per cent of the ocean floor is covered by seagrass beds they probably absorb ten per cent of the oceans' carbon dioxide. And since carbon dioxide is one of the main greenhouse gases, the large sharks, by helping protect these so-called carbon sinks, help maintain the atmosphere's fine chemical balance.

The oceans, it seems, are in a precarious state. In theory overfishing could be stopped: when fisheries are closed down fish stocks recover. But this can only happen if all fisheries and all fishermen abide by regulations. The number of fish caught would have to be controlled and the proportion of discards hugely reduced. Illegal and destructive methods would have to be policed. To curb these kind of infringements looks just about impossible, except on a very small scale. Which means we carry on as normal with self-interest winning over the common good: the 'tragedy of the commons'.

"The concept of global warming was created by and for the Chinese in order to make U.S. manufacturing non-competitive."
Donald Trump November 2012

Unlike overfishing, climate change are not reversible.

For the past two centuries - since the Industrial Revolution began and fossil fuels started to surpass whale oil - greenhouse gases, like carbon dioxide that traps the earth's heat – has increased. CO_2's over-abundance has been caused, mainly, by burning fossil fuels and cutting down forests. The majority of climate scientists now agree that global warming - the greenhouse effect - is a man-made environmental catastrophe in the making.

Another greenhouse gas - and a thirty times more potent heat trapper than CO_2 - is methane. Also known as marsh gas, methane is set free when forests are cut down; is released from landfills as rubbish rots; is associated with livestock farming, particularly the flatulence of cattle; and, as temperatures rise and ice melts, is released from where it has been stored for thousands of years in so-called 'methane sinks': glaciers, ice cores and permafrost - the permanently frozen layer that lies under the soils and rocks of polar regions and on the highest mountains. These icebound methane storage are a remnant of the last ice age that ended nearly twelve thousand years ago (and whose beginning was over two and half million years ago) and cover twenty-four per cent of Earth's north polar region: the Arctic Ocean's coastal fringes, the coasts of Siberia, northern Norway, Iceland, Greenland and the north of North America,. But now that formerly permanently frozen ground is melting and releasing methane from where it has been stored over all those millennia.

Nitrous oxide (N2O) is another heat-trapping gas and man-made N2O – like CO2 - originates mainly from burning fossil fuels, and also from nitrogen based fertilisers. The amounts aren't large, but N2O is a heat trapper two to three hundred times more powerful than CO2, and, of all the greenhouse gases, is one of the longest lasting. Once in the atmosphere it will remain there for about one hundred and fifty years, which is no laughing matter, even if it is called laughing gas.

We might be able to prevent the rate of Earth's is warming, but we can never reverse it. There can be no turning back. And rising temperatures are also hard to slow down.

As the climate gets warmer, forest and bush fires become more common and release more CO2. But then there is less forest and less bush to absorb the carbon dioxide. And as seawater becomes warmer it too absorbs less CO2 and the world's largest carbon sink - the oceans - becomes less effective. On top of that satellite observations have shown an unexpected phenomenon: an oily film produced by marine plankton and bacteria is cutting the oceans' CO2 absorption by half. Called "the surfactant effect" the more temperatures rise the more the surfactant effect is likely to increase.

Meanwhile, on land, the soil (which normally holds more carbon than the plants that grow in it) and peatlands (that, although only cover just three per cent of the Earth, sequester twice as much carbon as all the world's trees) are becoming ever more impoverished by intensive farming which damages its structure and diminishes its capacity to hold carbon. Then temperatures increase even more; permafrost becomes less permanent; icecaps and glaciers shrink in size; and frozen ocean sediment begins to melt. Then, without the whiteness of ice to reflect heat back to space - called the albedo effect (from albus, Latin for white) - the opposite happens: the dark water absorbs most of the sun's energy. By reflecting back just ten per cent of the sun's heat a vicious circle is set up: the more ice melts the more Earth warms and the more ice melts.

Over the past century average global temperatures have risen by about 0.6°C (1°F) and sea temperatures by about 0.1°C (0.18°F). Although the temperature of the oceans has not risen as much temperatures on land - and even though neither figure seem particularly dramatic - the impact of warmer waters has already had some devastating consequences on marine life.

All forms of ocean life are acutely susceptible to a change in temperature, whether warmer or colder, and every organism has its ideal temperature. And so, for example, as seas become warmer, cold water fish move to cooler seas; warm water species spread out over larger areas; and the whales are likely to find their prey has moved away from familiar hunting grounds.

Once it was unusual to find squid in the North Sea but now Scottish fisherman are catching thousands of tons a year. Does this explain why, over a period of two weeks in February 2016, twenty-nine sperm whales washed up on North Sea beaches (six on the UK's North Sea coast and the others on the coasts of France, Holland and Germany)? Might the whales have been hunting squid who had been chasing their own prey (of small fish and shrimps) that were heading northwards in search of an ideal temperature? Was that how the twenty nine whales found themselves in unknown waters?

Since sperm whales are deep divers they like to live far out in the ocean where depths are several thousand feet. If they find themselves in relatively shallow waters – like the fifty to one hundred feet deep waters south of Dogger Bank in the North Sea – it seems likely that their echolocation pings back in such an unfamiliar way they become confused. According to some opinions the noise from sea traffic and oil platforms adds to their disorientation – and their beaching. Could it be that the warming of the oceans had been the catalyst for the whales' misfortune?

Even the slightest change in temperature can be catastrophic, especially for the particularly vulnerable corals. As the whales pass over the oceans' coral reefs they cannot miss the most visible indicators of climate change: a change in water temperature is turning some corals white, whitened by the white algae that live in their tissues and feeds them, and which, when coral polyps are stressed, they discharge. The whitening - this coral bleaching - doesn't necessarily mean the corals are dead, but it can stunt the growth of these calcerous animals and make them more susceptible to disease.

In the Florida Keys, in January 2010, unseasonally cold water caused the corals there to bleach, but their bleaching was short lived and they recovered.

In 2106, off Queensland, north of Port Douglas, in the shallower waters of Australia's Great Barrier Reef, warming water caused bleaching that was so severe that an estimated seventy per cent of corals died. According to a study at the University of Queensland half of all Australia's Great Barrier Reef is already dead or dying and ninety-three per cent is bleached. Some scientists are predicting that in the next thirty years, ninety per cent of the world's corals will have died whether we halt global warming or not.

Could these doom-laden predictions be media hype? Or could this prognosis be based on misleading models of coral reef development? Or are we really seeing the beginning of the end of most tropical reefs? Only time will reveal the extent of their survival.

It is clear that Australia's 2016 and 2017 heatwaves had a catastrophic affect on the Great Barrier Reef. But in 2018 the temperatures were even higher – and there were fewer signs of heat stress. This suggests the survival of the tougher, more resistant, corals. If this is the case then it seems that some reefs can recover, albeit in a different state and supporting different species. And means that the humpbacks and dwarf minkes who travel through the Reef each winter are seeing changes that are more sudden and far reaching than their forbears ever saw.

Antarctica is Earth's most southern continent. On this ice-covered landmass, that is twice the size of Australia, the cold is so intense that the average surface temperature is -37°C. Hardly ever does it rain or snow, and if it does it never melts and so all its precipitation has been building up, frozen layer upon frozen layer, for over one and a half million years This is Earth's oldest ice and Earth's largest frozen mass: ninety per cent of the planet's ice is here and seventy per cent of its fresh water is locked in the continent's ice sheets, icebergs and glaciers. Underneath are mountains and valleys. Some are well below sea level, pressed down by the weight of one and a half miles of ice above. Nevertheless, even here, on Earth's coldest continent, ice shelves are thinning and glaciers are flowing faster.

Antarctica's mildest part is the Western Peninsula that juts out into the Southern Ocean. Roughly the size of California, and covering about four per cent of this coldest of continents, the Peninsula is one of the fastest warming areas on Earth. Since 1950 temperatures here have risen about about five times more than the 0.6°C world average. This is where, in summer and autumn, humpbacks come to feed. Their favourite places are the fjords where krill swarms are particularly dense. Minkes also come for the krill but they tend to prefer winter when they feed at the ice edge.

But Antarctic krill numbers have been falling, down by twenty per cent from what they were thirty years ago, and the reasons are not clear. Since sea-ice supports the ice-algae that are the krill's main food stock, it could be that the change in krill numbers is due to a loss of ice.

On the other hand krill also feed on phytoplankton that in theory should thrive where there is less ice - as less ice means more sunlight, and more sunlight means more energy for the microscopic marine algae to photosynthesise. But recently it has been found that although phytoplankton blooms are increasing in Antarctica's colder south, in the north of the Peninsula they are not only dwindling, but the phytoplankton there are now smaller-celled and less nutritional. This change is of no benefit to krill but it is ideal for salps, jellyfish-like creatures that can develop into swarms so vast they sometimes even outnumber krill. But as salps are mostly water they lack the high-quality protein content of krill that the whales depend on for survival.

There is yet another strand to the krill story. Two things are crucial for successful krill reproduction: timing and temperature. These tiny crustaceans lay their eggs in summer in surface waters and the eggs sink to where the water is the right temperature for hatching. The hatched larvae then swim back to the surface to feed on phytoplankton. But the newly hatched krill must feed in ten days, or die. That means unless phytoplankton develop at the same time as the hatchlings' rise to the surface the newly hatched krill have nothing to feed on. It's also vital that krill - both adult and hatchlings - feed well. They need to be fat enough to survive the winter as they graze the ice algae and shelter under the sea ice which also acts as a nursery.

The consequences of a plummeting krill population could be extremely serious: it could bring about the destabilisation of the Antarctic food web. If this happened then the whales who summer in northern Antarctica might have to travel six hundred miles further south to feed. Not only would they have to use more energy to get there, they would also have to take in more feed in a shorter season.

But there is more to Antarctica's problem than a potential shortage of krill and a fall in the quantity and quality of phytoplankton. The warming currents are sweeping warmer, sub-polar air across the region. At the same time the Antarctic Circumpolar Current (which normally acts as a barrier and keeps milder currents at bay) is itself warming. But the North Antarctic winds – which are always stronger than the winds further south – are being made stronger still by the warming currents. Since wind affects ice-free ocean surfaces more than those that are iced over they make a particular impact in summer when the ice recedes almost as far as the coast line. And these winds - depending on their strength - can have two effects. Either the disturbed water might carry nutrients to the surface. Or, if the winds are particularly strong, they might push phytoplankton down to where there is less light for photosynthesis. Strong winds also bring more cloud cover and that too means less sunlight for phytoplankton to convert to energy. And so, it seems, the southern pole is becoming ever more affected by large weather systems that drive winds to the ends of the Earth.

Meanwhile in the northern hemisphere, every year in March when spring comes to the North Atlantic and the water gets warmer, the world's largest phytoplankton bloom begins to spread northwards. Eventually it extends in a twelve to fifty mile band up to where the ice begins. For the animals who have, over millions of years, adapted to the Arctic's natural cycles of light and temperature its timing is crucial. For the zooplankton the bloom is a vital source of energy, just as zooplankton are an essential source of calories for those in the food chain above, including the great whales.

But Arctic temperatures are rising even faster than those at the South Pole (except for Antarctica's Western Peninsula). They are increasing at twice the current global rate and the Arctic sea ice ecosystem is, like the Western Peninsula, also changing. The metre-thick sea-ice is melting and sunlight is reaching parts it never has before. A transformation is taking place: changes that benefit some species, but not others.

More light means more sun-fed phytoplankton. That means plenty of food for the tiny zooplankton, like amphipods and copepods, that krill feed on and who also eat phytotplankton and other zooplankton that are even smaller than they are. It's also good for herring, who eat only plankton; and for capelin, who feed on krill and other small crustaceans; it's good for mackerel who feed on any fish that are smaller than themselves, including small mackerel. In turn the fish are eaten by the sea birds, the seals, the young walruses and the beluga whales that polar bears feed on. More sunlight is also good for predatory fish that hunt by sight. But it is not so good for species who have adapted to the dim light beneath the metre thick ice. The unfamiliar sunlight is likely to make them easy prey.

For the great whales who come in summer to feed on the polar krill (whose fat content is higher than krill at lower latitudes) the consequence of warming seas could be good feeding. But polar natives - like narwhals, beluga whales and ringed seals - who need a decent layer of fat to survive life in the northern extremes could have a problem. They like to feed on Arctic fish such as the one foot long Arctic cod that are high in fat and calories. But if, as the water warms, the less nutritious Atlantic fish keep moving northwards and the polar whales and seals eat those instead, they will have to catch more fish to gain the same energy.

But the diminishing ice cover means the Arctic fish also have a problem. Like all the animals that are part of the polar food chain they too depend on the algae that grows underneath the ice, that first link in the polar food chain that feeds the copepods that feed the smaller fish that sustain the Arctic fish.

Melting ice, by releasing fresh water, causes another problem. Since non-saline water is lighter than seawater it tends to lie on the ocean's surface where it can prevent the deeper nutrient-rich water from coming to the top. If that happens there could be insufficient nutrients for phytoplankton to thrive which would mean less nourishment for zooplankton, including the Arctic's most abundant grazing copepod: Calanus hyperboreus.

Hyperboreus means 'of the extreme north'. These minuscule Arctic crustaceans – that are about the size of a grain of rice, and whose body mass can be eighty per cent fat - have been described as the oceans' avocado, and also the Arctic's most important animal. Just as these extreme northern copepods depend on phytoplankton, so amphipods – tiny crustaceans about one third of an inch long, depend on them. And so the copepods – via the amphipods - pass their fat up the Arctic food chain to, among others, the Arctic fish and great whales.

But Calanus hyperboreus are vulnerable. Unlike all other copepods whose eggs are protected by a shell, the eggs of these Arctic zooplankton are covered only by a thin permeable membrane. Their lack of a protective chalky carapace makes them particularly susceptible to pollutants. Even very small amounts of petroleum oil can affect their hatching rates - which means that mining for oil in the Arctic, which holds the world's largest untapped gas and oil reserves, could have catastrophic consequences. Already the Norwegians have begun drilling in the Barents Sea north of Norway; the US are planning to expand offshore oil and gas exploration in the US's Arctic region, Alaska; and the Russians, who are already drilling under the Laptev Sea, are planning to do the same in the Barents and Kars Seas.

The retreating sea ice is causing problems for others too. The polar whales - the bowheads, narwhals and belugas - who have evolved to live at Earth's northern extremes are finding their habitat shrinking. In the last thirty years summer ice has fallen by half.

In February 2018, for the fourth consecutive year, temperature records in the Arctic were broken. At the most northern point of mainland Greenland, at Cape Morris Jesup four hundred and fifty miles from the North Pole, where the sun had not risen for four months, at what is normally the coldest time of the year, at a time when the ice sheet is usually still expanding, temperatures rose to 10°C above normal. At the same time Western Europe was being hit by the 'beast from the east' and it snowed in Rome. One explanation is that the polar vortex (the low pressure weather system that rotates anti-clockwise in the stratosphere five miles above the pole) had shifted (itself having possibly been destabilised by the warming of the stratosphere) and the shift allowed warm air to move north and cold air to move south.

If present trends continues it's possible that, by 2040. the Arctic could have no summer ice at. In theory, ships could sail over the North Pole. Compared with travelling through the Suez Canal sailing over the top of the world would cut the distance between northern Europe and north-east Asia by two fifths. But, given the lack of ports and the prospect of raging storms, this seems unlikely.

But it has become possible to sail round the Arctic ice-cap. For centuries explorers tried to discover the Northwest Passage, the Arctic route between the Atlantic and Pacific oceans. It took three years – from1903 – 1906 – for Roald Amundsen to make the first complete passage. But it wasn't until 2009 that the sea ice had retreated enough to allow regular traffic. Now it joins the Northeast Passage, along the coasts of Norway to Russia to the Pacific Ocean. The circuit is open for business and the new Arctic shipping lanes have become the latest lucrative trade routes.

But whether the native 'ice whales' will be able to tolerate the temperatures of the warmer seas that have opened up these new shipping lanes is not certain. What is certain is that polar bears and walruses will be without ice platforms to hunt from and have nowhere to build dens to breed in. Ringed seals, who also give birth in snow-covered lairs on top of the sea ice, will lose their breeding grounds too. Can they adapt to moving ever further north where the days are darker for longer? And what will happen if there is no summer ice at all, the ice that is itself an entire ecosystem? To answer these questions observations and evidence are necessary, but in the polar regions research is both expensive and difficult and, as a result, much about this extreme environment is 'data deficient.'

"Possibility is the oxygen on which hope thrives."
Paul Rogat Loeb, *The Impossible Will Take a Little While:*
A Citizens' Guide to Hope in a Time of Fear

The Oceans' oxygen has two main sources: the atmosphere and photosynthesis, mainly by phytoplankton. In water oxygen dissolves (as do the other atmospheric gases such as nitrogen and carbon oxide) and changes into the form that fish and plants - like seaweeds, seagrass and phytoplankton – breathe, and organic materials use to decompose.

The oceans' oxygen levels have always varied and there have always been 'oxygen minimum zones'. Normally they begin six hundred and fifty feet below the surface and are prevented from getting too big by the currents that transfer oxygen from the surface waters down to the cooler, dense waters beneath. But warming waters are slowing some currents' which means the upper and lower layers are mixing less. As a result some oxygen minimum zones are expanding - some by about three feet a year - and the top layer, the so-called mixed layer where oxygen is concentrated, is declining.

And so the race for oxygen is on. Already, off Central America's Pacific coast, an oxygen shortage has driven smaller shoaling fish - like sardines, herring and mackerel - closer to the surface. For the same reason their predators have been driven there too, large fish like, sharks, tuna and sailfish. And so the prey-predator dynamic has changed. For whales and a host of other marine animals who prey on smaller shoaling fish, the oxygen shortage has brought easy prey. But for commercial fisheries, who find their catch diminished, the changes are not so good.

"Look to the future because that is where I am going to spend the rest of my life"
George Burns, American entertainer

One third of the carbon dioxide that is released into the atmosphere is absorbed in the oceans - and levels are rising. When CO_2 is mixed with water their mixing sets up a chemical reaction that forms carbonic acid. In the past two hundred years the composition of seawater has changed more quickly than any changes in the previous fifty million years. The consequences are serious and are the reason why ocean acidification is often referred to as "climate change's equally evil twin".

Shell building animals need to absorb elements - such as nitrogen and phosphorus - to convert to calcium carbonate to form shells, and corals need similar components to build their skeletons. But too much acid in the water prevents these animals from taking in those elemental building blocks which means that as the oceans become more acidic the more the growth of these so-called 'marine calcifiers' is stunted.

A rise in the oceans' acidity is particularly bad news for a huge number of animals. As well as for reef-building corals it's bad for molluscs, such as whelks, mussels and clams; and echinoderms like sea stars and sea urchins; and crustaceans such as lobsters, crabs, barnacles and krill; and, at the very bottom of the food chain, it's bad news not only for krill but krill's own food source zooplankton that include copepods, the predominant members of the zooplankton world and probably the most abundant animals on earth.

But ocean acidification does more than inhibit shell forming. It seems to interfere with krills' ability to hatch, and also reduces the nutritional value of these calcifying animals. When shellfish were put in the kind of conditions that are expected by the end of the century the results showed that the way the animals collected and stored energy had been altered, and as a consequence their protein and fatty acid content had been much reduced.

It looks as if the acid content of the oceans has increased by about thirty per cent since 1751. With man-made CO_2 emissions still rising the future for marine calcifiers is not looking good. Unless carbon dioxide emissions are stabilised (an unrealistic hope according to some scientific opinion) the acidity of the oceans will reach a critical point when animals must adapt, or die.

Adaptation is not impossible. Some marine species have adapted to highly acidic environments, like those that live around hydrothermal vents. But they have evolved over millions of years. Unless the shell-forming animals that live in less extreme environments can adapt to the oceans' increasing acidity with unprecedented speed, might they be replaced with the kinds of acid-tolerating algae, sea grasses and small marine worms that surround oceanic volcanic vents?

Fish are also effected by a change in the oceans' acidity. Even small changes in the acidity of human blood can cause comas, seizures and death. Fish that have excess acid in their blood use extra energy to excrete it, energy that would be better used for hunting, escaping predators and digesting food. It also seems that a rise in acidity affects the way the brain processes information, and also slows growth and impairs the sense of smell and hearing, at least in sharks and clown fish on which studies have been done. Clown fish seemed unable to smell their way back to the particular type of sea anemone in which they live (and whose stinging tentacles protect them).

It seem the consequences of rising acidification could mean a rearrangement of prey species and, inevitably, repercussions for marine food chains.

"Anyone who believes in indefinite growth on a physically finite planet is either mad or an economist"
Sir David Attenborough

Not only has a change in sea temperatures seem to have changed the distribution of prey and driven some whales to hunt elsewhere; warming seas are also allowing invasive species to thrive in places they never could before.

The most obvious are algal blooms. Formed from microscopic single-celled algae, a type of phytoplankton, they can develop into thick, floating mats that can develop at a runaway pace. The largest cover tens of square miles and show up clearly on NASA's satellite data. Some have devastating affects - though not all.

But for blooms to grow the conditions have to be right. They need warmth, sunlight and nourishment. Nourishment comes from several sources. Some are natural, like ocean upwellings that bring nutrient-rich waters to the surface. Others are man-made. The most usual are nitrogen and phosphate, the run-off from fertilisers that are spread on crops on land. But anything that contributes to an oversupply of nutrients – such as dung from livestock, dead animals, sewage, or rotting vegetation - can create the ideal conditions for any of three hundred types of algae to grow – and bloom - at an alarming pace.

Algal blooms come in an array of colours, from green to yellow, brown, black or red. And they usually get a bad press. But not all are as destructive as the media would have it - like the North Atlantic's vast springtime bloom that feeds both the zooplankton and the great baleen whales.

But forming the basis of a multitude of marine food chains is not phytoplankton's only vital function. The importance of these small drifting plants cannot be overestimated. Not only are they indispensable major greenhouse-gas processors, but like trees on land are primary photosynthesisers, and suppliers of at least half of Earth's oxygen: "the oceans' green machines".

However, not all blooms are beneficial. At their worst 'harmful algal blooms' produce toxins that can be lethal and overwhelming. Though not for all. Some fish and shellfish are not in the least affected by eating toxic algae, but their predators – including whales and humans – can be severely poisoned as the toxins pass up the food chain.

Although blooms existed long before humans made any impact on Earth, and although now, in this, our anthropocene epoch, harmful blooms represent just two per cent of all these types of blooms, their range is spreading. As sea water warms, the oceans' acidity and salt levels change and in the changed conditions some toxin-producing algae that have been lying dormant in sediments, are suddenly able to thrive. As a consequence coral diseases have increased in recent years and so have harmful blooms. It seems likely that they will become even more intense and longer lasting than the bloom that developed on the United States' west coast in 2015, and was one of the largest ever recorded.

The so-called 'red tide' spread all along the Pacific coast from Mexico in the south to Alaska in the north. This particular type of algae produces highly toxic domoic acid, a powerful and potentially fatal neurotoxin that will be familiar to humans who have had amnesic shellfish poisoning. In normal circumstances the biotoxin is not dangerous, but concentrated in a bloom it accumulates in shellfish and small fish - like sardines and anchovies - who pass it up the food chain. In 2015 fisheries from California to Washington had to be shut down. Seals were found having seizures and foaming at the mouth. And dolphins gave birth prematurely – all symptoms associated with domoic acid poisoning.

It was once thought that the waters off Alaska were too cold for toxic algal blooms. But after the 2015 bloom domoic acid was found in marine mammals all along Alaska's coast, including whales and dolphins. Sea-birds were seen looking half-starved which suggested their food source had also been affected. That year, between May and August, the beaching of thirty dead whales - including fourteen finbacks, eleven humpbacks and one grey – was three times above the annual average. The increase was linked to the United States' bloom.

Not only do toxic blooms seem to be on the increase but it looks as if they are developing in places they never have before – including the Arctic. As the ice melts sunlight is able to penetrate the water and then plants and bacteria that ice cover rendered inactive are able to photosynthesise and thrive. This could explain why, off Greenland, domoic acid has been found in bowhead and beluga whales, and also in fur seals.

At the other end of the world, on the southern tip of South America off the Chilean coast, in May 2105 (the same year as the red tide spread along North America's Pacific coast) another toxic red tide killed twenty five million farmed salmon. About seventy per cent of the dead fish were thrown into the sea and it's thought that this so-called 'environmental crime' exacerbated the bloom which developed into the worst toxic red tide in history. It ravaged the fishing industry and compelled the government to declare Chile's south coast an emergency zone.

Later that same year a National Geographic observation plane flew over a remote and inaccessible fjord in the Chilean part of Patagonia. By chance, it spotted three hundred and seven decaying sei whales. It was one of the largest whale strandings on record, and it seems likely that the toxic red tide had been the cause of their deaths.

Although not all blooms are the consequence of human activity those that do usually cause most havoc.

But it is not just living blooms that can have lethal consequences. As the algae grow at an uncontrollable rate some die and the dead algae give new algae all the more to feed on. Some blooms live for days; others for months. And some, when they begin to decay, give off toxic gases. This is what happened on South Africa's west coast in St Helena Bay in 1994. A vast dying bloom turned black and over two thousand tons tons of fish and shellfish - fifty different species - died from hydrogen sulphide poisoning.

An algal mat is another name for a phytoplankton bloom and seems a more fitting description with its connotations of a dense, tangled, interwoven mass. Only when the dissolved oxygen supply in the water is eventually used up do algal mats turn brown and sink to the ocean floor where they find a new supply of oxygen. The oxygen re-activates decomposition and bacterial growth thrives again, only stopping when the final, revitalizing, supply of oxygen has been used up. When this happens the benthic species that can, flee, and those that can't, die. Having killed off all remaining organisms the dying blooms have created a dead zone.

Blooms come and go but dead zones last much longer. The largest ever recorded is in the Gulf of Mexico The size of the bloom fluctuates with water temperature and the pollutants that sustain it, but generally it covers nearly nine thousand square miles.

"The absence of evidence is not evidence of absence"
*Attributed to William Cowper, 18th century English poet
and Martin Reed, English astronomer
and Carl Sagan, American 'popular astronomer'*

As sea water warms it becomes less dense and expands; then, taking up more space than cool water, sea levels rise.

In the past hundred years sea levels have been measured by gauging tide heights and, more recently, by assessing data from satellite images. Several things - like tides, winds and salinity - cause sea levels around the world to vary. But on average, Earth's seas have risen by about eight inches since the beginning of the twentieth century,

Some computer models have shown that for every 1°C increase in global temperature - which is the extent Earth's temperature has risen since the Industrial Revolution began - sea levels will rise about eight feet. There is data that shows a rise of 4 °C would raise sea levels to between over twenty and thirty-five feet. But the change won't be instant. It could take a few hundred years, or a few thousand. Or less – depending on how quickly the polar ice sheets melt. But even if greenhouse gases are stabilised, because of the lag time, global temperatures will continue to go up and sea levels will inevitably rise.

Not all scientists accept such gloomy scenarios about climate change and rising sea levels. Some think the computer models are based on false premises and so make the predicted outcomes misleading. Those who question their accuracy are listed on Wikipedia: "List of scientists who disagree with scientific consensus on global warming". The list is long, but not as long as the ninety-seven per cent of scientists who believe the Earth is warming; that the warming is caused, mostly, by humans; and that only human intervention can change and control the environmental conditions we have created.

Thirty per cent of the world's population live in low-lying coastal areas. What if the Intergovernmental Panel on Climate Change's projection of a one metre sea level rise by 2100 does happen? Already eight Pacific Islands have disappeared. How many major cities could go the same way? A 3 °C rise could tip the balance for cities that have been built below sea-level, cities like Amsterdam, Jakarta and New Orleans. And what about those not far above the current sea-level, like Osaka, Alexandria, Rio de Janeiro; Shanghai, Miami, London - and many, many more.

"Futurology always ends up telling you more about your own time than about the future."
Matt Ridley *The Rational Optimist: How Prosperity Evolves*

Yet another concern about warming oceans is the possibility of disturbing the oceans' deep water currents. Collectively known as the Global Ocean Conveyor Belt together they form an ocean circulation system that loops around the planet – a great oceanic network that plays a crucial part in influencing Earth's climate. Flowing like vast rivers, driven by the wind and differences in water density, these all-important currents transfer heat, salt, nutrients and oxygen all around the globe.

The Northern Hemisphere loop of the ocean conveyor belt – and the world's greatest deep-water current - is known as North Atlantic Deep Water. It begins near Greenland and Norway where freezing water expels most of its salt. Then the unfrozen water, now dense and heavy with salt and cold, sinks, and in its sinking forms an underwater current. Very slowly this huge body of water is pushed southwards along the seabed until it reaches the other end of Earth, Antarctica, and joins the Antarctic Circumpolar Current.

Driven by the Southern Oceans' strong westerly winds the Antarctic Circumpolar Current is Earth's largest and strongest wind-driven current, hence its other name the West Wind Drift. Moving anticlockwise at two and a half miles an hour and three thousand feet deep it circles Antarctica in a twelve and a half thousand mile loop. The current has two main functions: it stops warm, northern air reaching the South Pole region; and carries North Atlantic Deep Water back towards the north.

The round trip takes five hundred years and as it travels its water continually turns over the oceans' distinct layers: the bottom, nutrient-rich, layers that lie on the seabed and include decomposed plant and animal matter; and the top layer that absorbs gases like carbon dioxide and oxygen from the atmosphere, and light and warmth from the sun. By bringing warm water northward and cold water towards the tropics, the

Global Ocean Conveyor Belt distributes warmth, salt and nutriments between the basins of the Atlantic and the Indian and Pacific Oceans and so plays a key part in keeping Earth's climate, and the oceans' ecosystems, stable.

Only one ocean, the Atlantic, transports heat northwards across the Equator. From the South Atlantic the Gulf Stream, a warm, salty, fifty mile-wide current travels northwards at three miles an hour (which is speedy for a current). When it reaches its northern point in the North Atlantic, and having completed its journey round the world, it sinks and drives North Atlantic Deep Water back towards Antarctica. There is concern that if unprecedented amounts of fresh water were released from the melting of Greenland's ice sheet this circumnavigating current could be weakened. If this were to happen, then the North Atlantic, south of Greenland, between Canada and Britain, would become colder.

Some scientists believe there are signs that this might already be happening. In the mid-Atlantic, between December 2014 and February 2015, the USA had a particularly cold winter and temperature and early snowfall records were broken all over the continent. Yet, at the same time the global average temperature reached a record high, as it did again in 2016. And the following year, 2017, was the second warmest on record.

Were is not for the Gulf Stream, the surface ocean current that carries water from the tropics to northern, cooler latitudes, Western Europe's temperature would be similar to North America's. Its southern counterpart is the Brazil current, but being weaker and shallower than the Gulf Stream it effects the climate less. But what does have far more impact on Brazil's climate - and much of the world's - is El Nino, which, of all the world's natural weather events is one of most influential.

Every two to seven years, in the tropical Pacific Ocean, a climate cycle is set off by an interruption to the trade winds. This usually happens in December, hence its better known name El Nino (Spanish for 'the boy child' Jesus, or, more fully, the El-Nino-Southern Oscillation). Normally the trade winds blow in an eastward direction. But sometimes the winds die out or go into reverse. When that happens then the east Pacific becomes unusually warm as winds, that are now from the west, push warm surface water eastwards towards South America.

The warming of the east Pacific sets up atmospheric circulation patterns that connect the tropics with mid latitudes. Their effect on weather conditions all over the world can be devastating: droughts in the Brazilian Amazon, in the north eastern United States, in Asia, east Africa, Australia and Indonesia. Heavy rains and floods in parts of South America. Winter storms in the south eastern United States. Snow and rain in normally dry regions of Peru, Chile and Mexico. And mass coral bleaching on Australia's Great Barrier Reef.

But El Nino can bring benefits to some. Fewer hurricanes in the north Atlantic. A milder winter in the northern United States and southern Canada; rain to replenish reservoirs in the south western United States; and in south eastern Africa drier weather reduces outbreaks of malaria.

La Nina is El Nino's exact opposite and is linked with below average sea temperatures and contrary types of weather. Both these weather events usually last twelve months, but sometimes, much longer. Normally El Ninos occur every two to seven years, and La Ninas every twenty-three years. But there are some atmospheric scientists who believe that global warming is causing La Ninas to occur at thirteen year intervals rather than their normal twenty-three year cycles.

Also in the eastern Pacific it seems that warmer, lighter water is pushing the thermocline - the thin layer that separates the surface waters from the deep waters – deeper. When this layer – between the top mixed waters and the calm, cold deep water - is pushed too deep it stops the upwelling of cooler, nutrient rich water. Then phytoplankton decline. The food chain is disrupted. All kinds of marine life find feed in short supply. And the great whales are among those who have to hunt elsewhere.

To date the hottest years on record are 1972-73; 1982-83; 1997-98; and 2015-16. There is concern that the combination of man-made climate change and natural climate cycles are taking the world into a hotter phase – with the poles warming fastest of all.

Once it was thought the main reason for the poles' speed of warming was due to the loss of the albedo effect, the reflection from the ice that sends about fifty per cent of the sun's energy back to space. But now it's thought that changes to the Earth's large weather systems might have more influence - the systems that have themselves been changed by rising temperatures, a rise that initially seems to have been partly caused by the lessening of the albedo effect.

And the world said "Does anyone else have plastic bags full of plastic bags or is it just me?"

So much to do with the Oceans is a mystery. Ninety-five per cent of the seafloor is, so far, unexplored and it's likely there are millions of species yet to be identified - and about a quarter of those in the uncharted waters of the deepest ocean, or so it is supposed. But how many creatures will become extinct without ever having been identified? We know more about the vast amount of plastic rubbish in the oceans than we know about the ocean bed and the huge number of organisms that live there.

Of all the plastic that is thrown away about, forty percent has been used only once; the so- called "disposables" such as cups, plates, cutlery, cigarette butts, cotton buds, tampon holders, plastic bags, bottles, food containers. The list goes on. And on.

Plastics are now amassing in such vast quantities that there could already be enough to form a permanent layer in the fossil records – the records that tells geologists so much about the history of the earth and paleontologists so little. Since mineralized bones are just a tiny fraction – only 0.01per cent - of all the species that have ever existed all fossilologists have to go on are mostly marine invertebrates and a few dinosaurs, a hugely incomplete representation of the whole line-up.

If plastics do eventually join the layered structures of Earth's history an ominous circle will have been completed. First came fossil fuels, the mineralised organic remnants of a geological past. Then they were extracted to become the raw materials for a plethora of synthetic, plastic objects. Finally abandoned, we have strewn the discarded remains of our plastic dependence into all Earth's oceans and over its land masses, to be laid down once again, only this time already in inert, inorganic form.

When thirteen male sperm whales were beached near the German town of Toenning. in 2016 the lethal effect of plastic was clear. The whales were probably between ten and fifteen years old and probably part of a bachelor pod. It seemed they had been starving as they were half the weight they should have been. But their stomachs were full − full of man-made plastic debris including a forty-three foot long fishing net and a twenty-eight inch piece of plastic from a car. It's likely they died of heart failure, brought on by starvation.

But it's not only toothed whales (like sperm and bottlenose whales - who gulp down their food without chewing) that are killed by marine rubbish. Filter-feeding, baleen whales are no less at risk. The death of a stranded Bryde's whale near Cairns in Australia had several witnesses who described her death as "agonising". An autopsy showed her stomach had been packed with six square metres of plastic rubbish including plastic bags and food packages.

We know that ingesting plastic kills. And we know from mariners who witness their plight, and from the scars on beached whales, that entanglement in plastic debris is also common. But what we cannot do - since most carcasses don't wash up on shore − is make any reasonable estimate of the death toll. It's not only the whales that die far out in the oceans and sink to the ocean bed. What about the scavengers who clear up their carcasses? Do they too get caught up in the fishing nets, ropes or strapping that might have killed the corpses they feed on? And do they too, having eaten the stomach contents, leave their meal with plastic in their own digestive systems?

When baleen whales feed on zooplankton that have themselves fed on toxic microplastics, the whales cannot but feed on the plastic pollution too. This is worse news for whales than it is for tiny drifting planktonic animals because the longer an animal lives the more toxins accumulate and the more concentrated they become.

The Mediterranean Sea is home to fin and sperm whales and six species of dolphin. It's thought that fin whales there could be swallowing several thousand pieces of microplastics every day. Some of the chemicals associated with these tiny plastic specks are known to damage digestive systems and alter hormones that regulate growth, development and reproduction. Only time will tell what the long term effects might be.

Most of the oceans' plastics – sixty percent is the calculation – now seem to come from China and South east Asia (from Indonesia, the Philippines, Thailand and Vietnam) which makes these countries the world's worst plastic polluters. And all as a consequence of their economic growth. It's also the reason why (according to a 2016 report by Japan's Environment Ministry) there is twenty-seven times more plastic in the seas around Japan than anywhere else on Earth.

Although it's well known that the Arctic is not immune from plastic incursion recent research has revealed concentrations two to three higher than previously recorded. Its unique plastic 'fingerprint' shows that most of this synthetic detritus has been driven northwards from the 'great Pacific garbage patch'. Its release from melting sea ice is also likely to be contributing to the plastic accumulation.

Once it was thought that Antarctica's continental shelf was almost untouched by mankind's pollution. But a Greenpeace survey, published in 2018, has shown that the Antarctic marine system has not escaped pollution from microplastics and hazardous chemicals. These are likely to have been carried, as they have been to the Arctic, by the winds and tides, or deposited by rain or snow. But not all the Antarctic pollution is in microscopic form. Floating debris – like buoys, nets and tarpaulins - has probably come from fishing boats, cruise ships and research vessels.

Even if dumper trucks could keep up with clearing all the world's coastlines, where marine trash is overwhelmingly plastic; and even if it was possible to clear all the plastics

160

floating on the oceans' surface and the seafloor, and even if we could clear up all the microplastics, our non-biodegradable plastic litter would still keep coming, coming from the construction industries; the packaging industries; the electronics, transport and clothing industries; from households and fast food outlets. Yet how can we manage without them?

To call the never-ending accumulation of non-biodegradable synthetic material a 'plastic plague' seems an apt description, though not in the sense of an epidemic caused by bacteria which eventually comes to an end, but in the sense of devastation on an overwhelming scale.

But remedies are being dreamt up and cleaning projects are in progress. International Coastal Cleanup is the world's largest volunteer initiative for removing plastic from beaches and waterways. Waste Free Oceans are encouraging the fishing and plastic industries to play a part in plastic management. And the non-profit organisation Ocean Cleanup, thanks to crowd funding, aims to make a start cleaning up the Pacific garbage patch in 2018. Using a fleet of fifty floating booms to collect the mass of debris they intend to bring it back to shore for recycling. If the computer models are correct the booms could clean up half the gyre in five years. To stop plastics reaching the seas in the first place there are also plans to place barriers in harbours and along coast lines. And there are proposals to manufacture less substantial plastic packaging; initiatives to cut down our use of plastic; and propositions about introducing deposits on bottles, based on the assumption that if one person throws one away someone else will it pick it up.

Some countries have put a total ban on plastic bags. Among them are China, Banlgladesh, India and several east and west African countries. Most European countries have taxed their use and so have some US states and some provinces in Argentina, Brazil, Chile and Colombia.

France is the first country to ban single-use cups, plates and cutlery. India has phased out non-recyclable, multi-layered plastic and encourages the use of plastic waste in road construction and energy production. Microbeads (used in cosmetics and cleaning products) have been banned in Canada, the UK, the US, the Republic of Ireland and the Netherlands.

We might hope that technology will come to the rescue. But given the scale involved, and the expense, the theory begins to look like a forlorn hope, other than on a very local scale. According to NOAA's Marine Debris Programme it would take sixty-seven ships one year to remove plastic from less than one per cent of the North Pacific. With the manufacture of plastics not letting up, and nineteen billions pounds of plastic entering the oceans every year, the supply seems eternal. And what of the main bulk of plastics, the microplastics that sink to the ocean floor, and are found even in ice cores and in the tiniest of marine organisms in the deepest parts of the ocean?

A more hopeful cure for our plastic addiction are bioplastics. Made from starch-based polymers found in plants they are biodegradable and their sources renewable. Corn is the main contender and the runners-up soya, sugar cane, beet and potatoes. Rabbit fur, sea grass, pineapple leaves are others. And so is bamboo - the world's largest grass and fasted growing woody plant. Its fibres make bioplastics that are particularly strong. Wood, or more precisely lignin - a polymer that keeps plants rigid and a by-product of paper mills - also makes impressively strong plastic. Recycled tomato pulp has been made into punnets; and egg-boxes have been made from a mix of rye grass and recycled paper. An Indian start-up has designed edible cutlery and chopsticks, made of rice, wheat and sorghum, that are baked rather than put through a complicated manufacturing process. Edible food packaging using milk protein, is at the research and development stage. But bioplastics can only decompose in temperatures of 50°C which could work on land, but not in the ocean.

But even if decomposable plastic is the future, the manufacture of non-renewable, fossil fuel-based polymers shows no signs of letting up other than on a very small scale. And the mountains of plastic already discarded are not going to disappear. We are sorely in need of plastic-degrading organisms - and the search is on. One of the more hopeful is a parasitic fungus, *pestalotiopsis microspora,* from the Ecuadorian Amazon that lives in the inner tissues of plants. This parasite is not only able to break down polyester and polyurethane but it can survive without oxygen which means it could, at least in theory, thrive deep down in landfills.

Another possible fix is mealworms (the larvae of the mealworm beetle that course fishermen use as bait). When a fisherman found that mealworms had eaten their way out of a plastic bag scientists were interested. Their research showed that when mealworm larvae feed they produce an enzyme that dissolves polystyrene. Larvae that were fed on a diet of Styrofoam were found not only to be as healthy as those on a normal diet (which is, usually, grains), but their waste (a biodegradable enzyme called ethylene glycoll) turned out to be as safe for growing crops as healthy soil. Even dead, mashed-up, worms produced the same polystyrene–dissolving enzyme. Although this prospect of transforming expanded polystyrene into organic material is directed at waste management on land it it's impact on the oceans could be considerable since eighty per cent of the oceans' plastic comes from the land in the first place, carried there by rivers, streams and wind: every year about eight million tonnes, equivalent to five full, rubbish sacks for every foot of coastline on Earth.

Initiatives that heighten awareness of the Ocean's plastic predicament are also growing. Sir David Attenborough called the 2016 movie *A Plastic Ocean* "The most important film of our time". In 2017 a catamaran, called Plastiki, made out of twelve thousand and fifty plastic bottles, sailed across the Pacific Ocean from San Francisco to Sydney. In Kenya an expedition is being planned to sail Flipflopi, a sixty foot dhow, made from flip-flops and recycled ocean plastics, to Cape Town. And other ocean plastics are being recycled to make high-end fashion garments like running shoes and sun glasses, beach huts and soap dishes, chairs and car bumpers, and, among many other things, bottles and carrier bags.

But how realistic are all these good intentions to clear up the mess we have made? Are they just a proverbial drop in the ocean compared to the mountains of plastic that have accumulated in our recent past, in less than a century, in not even eighty years - and seem impossible to eradicate? And what about all the plastic products that are still in the making?

Since fracking took off in 2010 in the United States, plastic's raw material, shale gas, has became even cheaper. Since then a boom in plastic manufacture has been in progress and a search for new markets is on. New facilities are being set up, and not only in the United States. America is busy exporting the raw materials for manufacturing new plastic products all over the world. Huge cargo ships are carrying containers filled with tiny, pellet-shaped nurdles to Europe (where Germany is the biggest plastic producer) and also to the Middle East and China.

Unless we take urgent measures to deal with it, Earth's plastic problem is expected to increase by thirty five per cent by 2025. And whales, who were once regarded as oil repositories, will become garbage receptacles, ingesting plastic by the ton, and also collectors of toxins that, once in their systems, could remain there forever.

Will plastic also become in increasing part of our diet as we too take in plastic fragments with the seafood we eat? A UK study estimated that seafood lovers ingested over two thousand plastic particles a year; a Belgian study calculated a much higher figure: eleven thousand particles a year. Though to find out which is right, and whether or not they are harmful, needs further research. Might we – though the whales cannot - have to look for food elsewhere?

"There are known knowns. These are things we know that we know. There are known unknowns. That is to say, there are things that we know we don't know. But there are also unknown unknowns. There are things we don't know we don't know."
Donald Rumsfeld, 2002, when he was the US's Secretary of Defence under George W. Bush

There is good news and bad news. Whale numbers are increasing. But the ocean's ecosystems are altering and the whales' world is changing.

Since the Oceans are Earth's greatest reservoir of heat there is cause for concern. According to NASA (the USA's National Aeronautics and Space Administration) our seas absorb ninety per cent of man-made increased warming. Scientific studies have assessed the amount of damage so far. And mathematical computer models - using data based on those assessments - project the future.

At international climate change conferences discussions are based mostly on climate models, or in other words, experimental evidence. The 2015 Paris Agreement set out to limit global warming to below 2°C. Some forecasters predict that if temperatures go up more than 2°C polar ice will melt even faster than it is melting now; sea levels will rise more quickly; the acidity level in the oceans will increase more rapidly; storms will become more frequent and more severe; there will be super droughts on land; and everywhere, mass extinctions.

But basing future outcomes - like climate change - on computer simulation depends on the detail. Even assessing the present has its difficulties, especially for extreme environments like the Arctic and Antarctic. That makes estimating the future harder still, and explains why research findings are so often fraught with contradictions. And although data collection and data analysing techniques are always improving that doesn't seem to bring about consensus either. Some commentators claim the impact of greenhouse gas emissions has been overstated and that doom-laden predictions based on climate change models are consistently wrong. Other estimations are more moderate. In 2017 studies carried out at the University of Washington led researchers to conclude that a 2°C rise was the best-case scenario. But comments on the prospect of keeping the temperature below 2°C vary from between "still possible" and "not a cat in hell's chance".

As we haven't got to 2°C yet we can't know for sure what will happen if we get to that point, or, as the more apprehensive climate scientists would have it, when. Will our climate become unpredictable and reek havoc? Some say the turmoil has already begun: that heat waves, droughts, floods, fires and storms are already more intensive and more frequent; that sea levels are rising; that the oceans are more acidic; and marine ecosystems are changing. The 2017study concluded that by 2100, the chance of an average global temperature rise of between 2°C and 4.9°C was ninety per cent likely. But that prediction depends on 'known unknowns' – among them the size of the future world population and the carbon output per person.

But what can't be disputed – because the figures relate to the past – is that since1880, when global temperatures were first recorded, Earth has warmed 0.8°C 1.4°F. And neither can the slowdown that happened during the fifteen years before 2014 (which was contrary to the rapid temperature increase that many models had predicted) be in doubt. Though to most climate change scientists fifteen years is a very short time in climate history. They say that this lower rate of change could be part of a far longer climate cycle.

Nevertheless the gainsayers insist a temperature rise of 2°C is hyperbole. They say climate models are unreliable, and that, in any case, a temperature rise of only a few degrees is nothing to worry about. They say animals and plants can adapt. That Antarctica is too cold for its ice to melt to any significant degree. That the rise in sea levels is exaggerated. That the IPCC (the Intergovernmental Panel on Climate Change) is alarmist. That climate change cannot be agreed until it is proven. That extreme weather events are normal. And that the more CO_2 increases, the more plants grow.

That raised levels of carbon dioxide increase plant growth cannot be doubted. NASA's satellite data shows that half of the world's vegetated space is becoming greener. Assessments have been made and the experts agree that an increase in CO_2 (together with sunlight and precipitation) has indeed increased the rate of photosynthesis and extent of plant growth.

But there is always a 'but'. Some climate models are showing that the increase in plant growth will diminish as plants acclimatise to the CO_2 increase; that an imbalance between nitrogen and carbon could cause crops to contain fewer nutrients such as iron, zinc and protein; and that the higher temperatures rise the drier growing conditions will become, and as a consequence any benefits from increased CO_2 will lessen.

Or could the opposite happen? Could more greening bring about a change in Earth's water cycle - and therefore the planet's climate system, and cause ever more extreme weather events? Then the effect on more greening could be a negative one. In other words, CO_2 is good for plant growth – but not necessarily in a beneficial way.

When it comes to the oceans' plant life the opposite is the case: NASA's instruments have shown that phytoplankton (which convert carbon into oxygen on a scale equivalent to plants on land) are diminishing. Though the data is sound the reasons for their decline are hypothetical though most are linked to the increase in greenhouse gases. CO_2 is the main contender but the other greenhouse gases - methane, nitrous oxide and ozone, together with man-made chlorofluorocarbons and hydrofluorocarbons - also absorb infrared radiation from the sun and so play a part in the oceans' rising surface temperatures. But things do not always turn out as expected.

In the North Atlantic a change has taken place that is baffling scientists. Coccolithophores are microscopic, photosynthesising, one-celled, plant-like organisms that are covered in about thirty limestone cells. Studies spanning forty-five years show these tiny algae are now ten times more numerous than they were at the beginning of the study. Since ocean acidification usually harms organisms like these stony plants that form shells from calcium carbonate, this is the opposite of what was expected to happen.

Although some very small fish feed on coccolithophores krill do not. Since1997 vast milky-blue blooms of these nutrient-limited microscopic plants have been appearing in the Bering Sea, and the krill population has been declining, a decline that could be a problem for, among many others, the whales who summer in this northern extreme of the Pacific Ocean.

On the plus side these photosynthesising forms of plankton play a crucial part in absorbing carbon. The relative weight of their shells helps them sink to the ocean floor in quantities so vast they are also known as marine snow. Accumulating over tens of millions of years they eventually become limestone: the chalky, white cliffs of Dover are a prime example.

Usually coccolithophores thrive in nutrient poor conditions where other forms of phytoplankton cannot. That makes their recent increase in the nutrient-rich Bering Sea another mystery. But there is much more to this puzzle than not knowing why the balance and distribution of some phytoplankton has altered. How do individual species react to rapid change? Why does ocean acidification harm some organisms- like corals, clams and some snails - but not others such as coccolithophores, or crustaceans, like crabs and lobsters? Unanswered questions like these show how little is known about the way so many of the oceans' complex ecosystems function.

Invariably researchers' claims are met by counter claims and often their findings depend on the researchers' interests. For instance, a marine biologist might take a different line from, say, an executive in the oil business. Or perhaps it suits some interested parties to think the worst when jobs, research funding and industries rely on the prospect of global warming. When a study was published that showed the more acidic sea water became the further sounds travelled, it didn't take long before three research papers were published that refuted that finding. They showed that most sound waves, rather than travelling for thousands of miles, are absorbed by the sediments on the seabed. The challenging analysis was funded by naval research.

"Hooray! Hooray! The end of the world has been postponed!"
Tintin in Hergé's *The Shooting Star*

In spite of the seemingly overwhelming task to cope with anthropogenic pollution, that is, pollution caused by mankind, a renewable revolution has begun. The purpose is to restore the equilibrium of Earth's climate and the plan is to put a stop to the rising temperature by cutting CO_2 emissions from burning, oil, coal and gas, and also forests and waste materials.

Limits have been set for carbon emissions, and quotas have been decided. For some experts this isn't enough. They think the only way to be in with a chance of curbing Earth's warming is for fossil fuel reserves to stay where they are: in the ground. Others agree we need to aim for zero carbon emissions: that we must halt all fossil fuel emissions and generate energy only from renewable sources such as wind turbines and solar panels. There are those who believe we have a ninety-three per cent of stopping temperatures rising, but only if greenhouse gas emissions are reduced by sixty per cent over the next ten years. And some who think the whole global warming scenario is hokum; that it is nothing at all worth worrying about; and that trying to fix what doesn't need fixing is a waste of time and money. But they are in the minority.

Nevertheless cutting down on our dependence on fossil fuel has begun. The goal is zero carbon emissions with all energy to be sourced from renewables - from wind, sun and hydro; from waves and tides; from geothermal power - from any power, as long as it is not generated from coal, oil or gas.

Many ideas for reducing our carbon use are familiar and depend on personal initiatives rather than industrial fixes. Cut back on long distance travel. Buy energy efficient gadgets. Have fewer children. Insulate buildings. Turn down central heating or air conditioning. Eat less meat. And, generally, aim for our rubbish to be reduced, reused or recycled.

Neither is there a shortage of ideas for technical fixes, though some seem extreme, such as fertilising the oceans with iron to increase plankton growth and so boost the absorption of carbon from the atmosphere. Or making artificial trees treated with chemicals (like sodium carbonate) that would soak up CO_2 considerably more efficiently than natural trees. Or set out banks of mirrors to deflect sunlight back to space. Or spread sulphur particles in the air to reduce sunlight, as erupting volcanoes do. (When Mount Pinatubo blew in 1991 the global average temperature declined by half a degree Celsius, and ice melt in Greenland was less than normal).

But these are risky, large-scale experiments that could trigger unintended consequences such as the destruction of ozone that, in the upper atmosphere, protects all living things from the sun's harmful, ultraviolet rays. Or increase acid rain that would exacerbate the oceans' acidification.

When it comes to food production innovation is prompted as much by climate change as the prospect of a burgeoning human population. The current world population is 7.6 billion - a three fold increase since the 1950s when it was 2.5 billion and our use of plastic was just beginning to become established. It looks as if it's on course to rise to 9.8 billion by 2050. Some statisticians are predicting that by 2100 human numbers will reach 12 billion. But others think 14 billion is more likely, almost double what it is now. But the further ahead the projections, the more likely they are to vary since calculations are based on the change of population over time.

But whatever the number, more people means more industry, more transport, more fishing, more deforestation, more agriculture, more livestock, more heating and cooling, and more greenhouse gasses. According to some opinions the maximum human population that the Earth could support is between nine and eleven billion.

One way of producing enough food to feed eleven billion people and at the same time curb the greenhouse effect could be to replace intensive agriculture with 'no-tillage', 'Conservation Agriculture'. The main purpose of Conservation Agriculture is to protect the soil from deep ploughing which not damages its structure and also releases CO_2 into the atmosphere. But this type of agriculture also improves soil structure by replacing monocultures - that is, planting the same crops in the same soil over and over again with crop rotation - that is, varying the types of crops that follow on from each other after harvesting. Not only has Conservation Agriculture been shown to increase crop yields, but keeping bare soil either planted or covered with crop residue protects it from erosion.

Also proposed is a reduction in meat consumption – for two main reasons. The first is that livestock are a major source of greenhouse gases. The second is that thirty three per cent of the world's agricultural land and one third of the world's fish catch is used to feed intensively farmed animals. With meat production on course to double by 2050 we are almost sure to run out of land to grow food and fish to fish. In other words we need to change to a short and efficient food chain – like that of the baleen whales whose main food source is zooplankton. Getting energy from the so-called primary producer means no energy is lost by being transferred through several links of a food chain. Instead it goes directly to the the top consumers, like humans and whales. For humans an equally short and efficient food chain would mean cutting out all the energy-consuming links in the factory-farming food chain. Instead we would eat directly what we grow on land, or catch at sea, rather than feeding ninety per cent of the world's soybeans, fifty percent of the world's grain and forty per cent of our wild-caught fish (as we currently do) to feed farmed animals, who having reached their slaughter weight have to be butchered, packaged and delivered, and in their processing emit still more greenhouse gases.

Other ways to produce meat and fish without the need for any feed at all are in the experimental stage. Known as 'cellular agriculture', using just a few cells as a starter culture, the flesh of any chosen species will be developed in laboratory conditions. The end product is intended to match the texture and taste, and possess all the same nutritional qualities, of the species it originated from. And as a consequence of the sterile conditions of its production, be uncontaminated by toxins.

There are too other ideas for feeding livestock (and pets): process maggots, the soft limbless larva of insects, for feed. The larva could be fed on waste from slaughterhouses and leftovers from supermarkets which, so this argument goes, would be a good way of making use of organic waste and would leave more land for growing food that humans can eat directly.

Or we could take up entomophagy ourselves (entomon is Greek for insect and phagein means "to eat") and eat insects directly. This might seem strange to some of us, but not to the

Chinese, Japanese, Mexicans, Tawainese and Australian aborigines for whom eating insects is perfectly normal. In some western countries a start has already been made and insect snacks are making inroads into niche markets They might not appeal to everyone but being high in protein and rich in iron, zinc and oil, they make nutritious eating.

The most recent development in entomophagy is insect oil. Processed from the larvae of the darkling beetle (that aficionados call a superworm) it's claimed that this oil is healthier than any vegetable oil on the market. Its other credentials are environmental. As a replacement for palm oil (that accounts for thirty per cent of the world's vegetable oil and is found in about half of all household products from cakes to detergents and fuel to cosmetics) it could have a huge effect in reducing deforestation and the destruction of habitats.

But whatever countermeasures are taken, a carbon-free world won't be cheap. All over the world energy use will have to have a complete makeover. Buildings will have to be transformed. Transport will have to be revolutionised; electric cars are already here; and the development of electrically powered shipping vessels and aircraft is underway. Billions will be made and billions spent.

Despite Donald Trump's intent to reboot the US's coal industry the US's renewable energy sector is steadily expanding. And China, the world's biggest air polluter, leads the world in producing electricity from renewable energy and is also the world's biggest investor in so-called renewables. All kinds of investment opportunities abound such as reusable, recyclable and compostable replacements for synthetic plastics; clothing from wood pulp; reverse vending machines (put in a bottle and get out a deposit); producing light from gravity; powering ovens with the sun; or generating electricity from fuel cells. But there seems to be a catch.

The technologies for a carbon-free future, like electric motors and solar panels, will themselves need energy to produce. They will also need a far greater range of metals than was used in the construction of their carbon-fuelled counterparts. Electric cars cannot function without cobalt for making lithium-ion batteries.

And solar panel manufacturers cannot produce photovoltaic cells without cadmium and tellurium.

And so, as the demand for fossil fuel decreases, the demand for metals will increase. We are going to need more aluminium and copper; more diamonds, gold and silver; more lead, more nickel, zinc.

On land these minerals are embedded in rocks and difficult and expensive to extract. But down in the depths of the oceans, usually near hydrothermal vents, they lie on the seabed in massive deposits.

Plans are in the making to send robots down to collect these base and precious elements from the oceans' deepest parts. Mining the deep-ocean floor is likely to be hugely profitable. It has been calculated that if all the gold that lies on the seabed were divided among all the people on Earth there would be £15,000 worth - nine pounds in weight - for every single person.

But extracting these highly prized deposits could effect thousands of square miles of deep-ocean floor. Disturbed sediments would smother habitats, destroy ecosystems and wipe out all manner of species. Toxic plumes would rise to the surface. Mining equipment would be noisy, and oil and chemical seepage unavoidable.

In the process of becoming carbon-neutral, at least initially, we are bound to use fossil fuels and emit even more carbon. And the end products - even if they ultimately help reduce our reliance on carbon - cannot but contain 'embodied energy', that is, the fossil fuel energy that was used not just in their manufacture but in every stage of their production: from the sourcing of raw materials – such as oil exploration and extraction, to the making all manner of goods and equipment; the energy used to transport and deliver them; to maintain and operate them; and, finally, when they are worn out - or replaced by more efficient models - the energy used in their disposal.

Since fracking took off in 2010 in the United States, plastic's raw material, shale gas, has became even cheaper. Since then a boom in plastic manufacture has been in progress. But shale gas has a hidden benefit. Being a far cleaner fuel than coal, the USA's CO_2 emissions are at a twenty-five year low - which shows there are other ways to cut greenhouse gas emissions other than international climate change agreements, like the international Paris Agreement which President Trump reneged on. Germany and Japan, who signed up to the Paris Accord, have invested heavily in renewables yet are consuming more coal than ever before. And CO_2 emissions in China – also a signatory – are, after a slowdown, again on the increase. As for poorer countries. The condition of their decreasing CO_2 emissions depends on payments from the richer economies, and they don't seem forthcoming

Over the last ten years global emissions of CO_2 have, on average, continued to grow by two and half per cent. With fourteen giant fossil fuel projects in the planning it seems there are no signs of that growth letting up. Massive research projects are currently in progress in the Arctic; in Canada and the US; in Brazil, Venezuela and Kazakhstan; in the Caspian Sea, Iraq, and Africa (where fourteen countries produce about fourteen per cent of the world's oil); and in China, Indonesia and Australia. If these are developed and all this coal is burnt CO_2 emissions could increase by twenty per cent. It seems that we are on course for business as usual.

And the world said "Are you sure you want to save the changes?"

But what do all these human impacts on the oceans mean for the whales: the oceans' warming and their increased acidification? The change in the distribution of prey? The ever-increasing pollution from plastics and lost fishing gear? The growth of shipping, the increase in commercial fishing, the expansion of harmful algal blooms? And more noise, more oil spills and more toxic chemicals?

The whales' world is vast compared with ours: ninety per cent of Earth's habitable space is in the oceans, and ninety-five per cent of Earth's water. Seventy-one per cent of the planet's surface is water - the water that makes Earth look blue from space, and makes it seem that Planet Ocean might be a more fitting name for the celestial body we inhabit than Planet Earth.

At its deepest the seabed is deeper than Mount Everest is high (the Mariana Trench, in the western Pacific Ocean, is about seven miles deep and Mount Everest's height is five and half miles). Apart from these extremes the ocean floor has features just like those on land: valleys, mountains, plains, plateaus, chains of volcanoes. Yet ninety-five per cent of this ocean habitat is so far unexplored and, possibly, two thirds of ocean life is yet to be discovered.

Although the whales seem to have a space that is immeasurably big their existence depends on the oceans' upper layers, the top six or seven hundred feet known as the euphotic, or "well lit" zone; the surface waters where sunlight reaches and plankton photosynthesise and thrive, and where most marine life lives.

Once it was assumed that deep down in the unlit darkness of the ocean depths no kind of marine life could possibly exist and that vast tracts of the seabed must be nothing more than barren wilderness, devoid of all life. But now we know that this is not the case at all. Down in the abyss, thousands of feet below the surface, where animals from the upper layer never venture (apart from sperm and beaked whales and the great white shark) there are all kinds of extraordinary creatures including strange sponges, jellyfish, tube worms, snails, crabs, urchins and fish. And also, it seems safe to assume, a host of animals yet to be discovered.

In contrast to the oceans dry land accounts for just twenty nine per cent of Earth's surface and it's a one dimensional place, a hugely more confined area than the vast depths of wilderness underneath the surface of the oceans. If you take into account that one third of land is uninhabitable and unproductive - being either desert, high mountains or frozen - it seems smaller still. And yet smaller when you think of a human population of over seven and a half billion that could get close to doubling by the end of this century.

Ever since the seas were first formed four billion years ago, mineral salts have been leaching out of the rocks and the rains have been washing them down to the oceans. These salts have changed the oceans' chemistry, just as anthropogenic pollutants also do.

But the oceans' salts have been accumulating in geological time – a time scale so great that it is counted in periods of millions, or billions, of years. And within these time spans, in step with the pace of evolution, marine life has slowly adapted and taken on characteristics to suit a gradually changing environment.

Man-made pollutants, on the other hand, have been increasing at a rate computable in mere decades, pollutants such as greenhouse gases in the atmosphere and industrial chemicals in the soil; contaminants that - since the oceans, land and air are inextricably linked - have no boundaries. A speed of change that, in the natural world, never happens so fast.

Most man-made pollution is insidious, potentially lethal and often invisible. By the time it becomes noticeable the damage has usually been done. Although nature is good at adapting it needs time. Already plants and animals are dying out at at ever quicker rates. Temperatures are rising and the climate is becoming less stable. Although life seems, at least for most of us in the developed world, to be continuing as usual, could it be that we have reached a critical point – the tipping point - the point of no return when man-made changes will be irreversible. Could it be that Earth's equilibrium has already become so destabilised that we are heading full-tilt for the next mass extinction?

In the last half-billion years life has nearly been wiped out five times. The first extinction, the Ordovician-Silurian, happened when most life was sea-life, four hundred and forty-three millions years ago. T he second, the Late Devonian Mass Extinction, began three hundred and seventy-five million millions years ago. In over fifteen million years three-quarters of all living creatures had gone. In the third, the Permian Mass Extinction, also known as the Great Dying, two hundred and fifty two million years ago, ninety-six per cent of all living things died out - and it's from the surviving four per cent that all of today's life has descended. The fourth, the Triassic-Jurassic extinction, two hundred million years ago spanned eighteen million years. Exterminations were slow then. But the fifth, the one that wiped out the dinosaurs, the Cretaceous-Tertiary – or K-T - mass extinction, was quicker. In less than two million years the dinosaurs were gone.

And now, in the Holocene - the current geological epoch which began when the last ice age was coming to an end nearly twelve thousand years ago - it looks as if the sixth mass extinction is underway. An extinction that could be the quickest of all. And the only one to be man-made, depending on whether you think the current extinctions are natural extinctions, or that nature is capable of fighting back. According to a World Wildlife report nearly of half of the oceans' populations have halved in forty years.

There are a number of biologists, geologists and paleontologists who feel sure that in a hundred years - due to pollution, habitat destruction, the incursion of invasive species and climate change - over half of all species presently living will be extinct. But other theorists feel just as sure that man-made global warming is a myth and that reports of the potential death of a mass of species have been exaggerated. They certainly don't agree with some reports that claim that every hour three species of either plants, insects, birds or mammals become extinct, a rate faster than any since the time the dinosaurs began to die out sixty-five million years ago.

American Paleontologist Doug Erwin is one of them. He is an expert on the End-Permian, the third great extinction when volcanoes nearly wiped out all life, two hundred and fifty-two million years ago. He acknowledges that humans have caused a great deal of damage, but says that those who think a mass extinction has begun don't understand what a mass extinction really is. To him the die out we are experiencing is nothing like a mass extinction that kills almost everything. But, says Erwin. if he is wrong, and the Sixth Mass extinction has begun, then there no point in trying to stop it.

Nevertheless there are many experts, including Sir David Attenborough, who believe an anthrocene (anthro for human and cene for ' recent') extinction has begun: an extinction triggered mainly by environmental pollution caused by human activity – a consequence of anthropocentrism: mankind believing we are the most important element of existence.

This Anthropocene extinction - or the present fall in wild populations, depending on your point of view - is being monitored – and found unusual. In previous extinctions size seems not to have made any difference. But in the present time it's the larger species that are dying out more quickly, those at the top of the food chain. Perhaps this is explained by the speed of today's environmental changes. Evolution has proved that quick alterations to the environment are not good for larger animals; for them gradual genetic changes give them the best opportunity for survival. But smaller species like marine algae - that multiply at a rate of several hundred generations a year - are likely to cope and thrive.

According to the World Wildlife Fund the past forty years have seen a thirty-nine per cent decline in marine populations, including sea birds. Nevertheless some whales – whose near annihilation also once happened at an unprecedented rate - are making a comeback. The question is whether they can adapt to the speed of the current changes.

Whatever happens global warming is not reversible – though, in theory, it is stoppable. But only just. We cannot just slam on the brakes. Even if we manage to put a halt to overfishing and decimating forests, and find alternatives to plastics, and generally slow down the rate of pollution, temperatures will continue to rise and ocean acidification will continue to increase, albeit at a slower pace. A recovery could happen. But it will take time. And it will take more than designated sanctuaries and marine protected areas to save the whales.

But what if climate change cannot be slowed? What if the acidity levels of the oceans keep rising at the present rate and animals that form shells, like zooplankton and krill, don't have time to adapt? And what if the number of animals at the top of the food chain also drop to a critical point, critical enough to set off a cascade effect, a network collapse?

In this worst case scenario larger fish would be replaced by smaller, plankton-eating fish. The plankton population, unable to cope with rising acidity would fall. And jellyfish - that are better able to tolerate acidic conditions, and also warmer temperatures, low oxygen levels and pollution - would thrive until, finally, the most common things in the ocean would be jellyfish and plastic rubbish.

Professor Stephen Hawking gave us one thousand years before viruses and global warming gets us, and thought that the only way for humans to survive would be to decamp to another planet.

Australian scientist Professor Frank Fenner reckons that we only have one hundred years before overpopulation, environmental destruction and climate change wipe us out.

But others – like those who work on global sustainability - think the development of wind and solar power is progressing at such a speed and on such a scale that their development can put us back on a more hopeful path.

There is a lot anthropogenic damage we can never repair. But if we aim to save as much of the whales' environment as we can, then we might be able to save ourselves - because if the whales can't survive, neither can we.

***

39097200R00101

Printed in Poland
by Amazon Fulfillment
Poland Sp. z o.o., Wrocław